Legends of the

MARTIAL
ARTS
MASTERS

Susan Lynn Peterson

TUTTLE Publishing

Tokyo | Rutland, Vermont | Singapore

ABOUT TUTTLE
"Books to Span the East and West"

Our core mission at Tuttle Publishing is to create books which bring people together one page at a time. Tuttle was founded in 1832 in the small New England town of Rutland, Vermont (USA). Our fundamental values remain as strong today as they were then—to publish best-in-class books informing the English-speaking world about the countries and peoples of Asia. The world has become a smaller place today and Asia's economic, cultural and political influence has expanded, yet the need for meaningful dialogue and information about this diverse region has never been greater. Since 1948, Tuttle has been a leader in publishing books on the cultures, arts, cuisines, languages and literatures of Asia. Our authors and photographers have won numerous awards and Tuttle has published thousands of books on subjects ranging from martial arts to paper crafts. We welcome you to explore the wealth of information available on Asia at **www.tuttlepublishing.com**.

These stories are works of fiction. All names, characters, places and incidents are fictitious or used fictitiously and should not be construed as accurate representations of actual persons, events, or locales.

First published in 2019 by Tuttle Publishing, an imprint of Periplus Editions (HK) Ltd.

www.tuttlepublishing.com

Copyright © 2019 by Susan Lynn Peterson
Illustrations © 2019 by Joe Reynolds

Library of Congress Control Number: 2019938431

ISBN 978-0-8048-5205-0
(Previously published as under ISBN 978-0-8048-3518-3)

First edition
22 21 20 19   5 4 3 2 1
Printed in China   1906CM

Distributed by

North America
Tuttle Publishing,
364 Innovation Drive,
North Clarendon,
VT 05759-9436 U.S.A.
Tel: 1 (802) 773-8930
Fax: 1 (802) 773-6993
info@tuttlepublishing.com
www.tuttlepublishing.com

Japan
Tuttle Publishing,
Yaekari Building,
3F, 5-4-12 Osaki,
Shinagawa-ku,
Tokyo 141-0032
Tel: (81) 3 5437-0171
Fax: (81) 3 5437-0755
sales@tuttle.co.jp
www.tuttle.co.jp

Asia Pacific
Berkeley Books Pte Ltd,
3 Kallang Sector #04-01,
Singapore 349278
Tel: (65) 6741-2178
Fax: (65) 6741-2179
inquiries@periplus.com.sg
www.periplus.com

To my martial arts teachers

Kandie Vactor, Tony Linebarger, Lend McCaster,

Johnny Linebarger, Jeff Zauderer, John Spooner, and

Bill Mailman, who over the years have taught me

far more than martial arts technique.

Contents

Acknowledgments

My thanks to all the people who made this book possible: To the folks of the CompuServe Writers' Forum, especially the Research and Craft section, for insights into everything from botany to bow strings, tigers to tofu. Thanks especially to section leaders Diana Gabaldon and Susan Martin, and to Jo Bourne, Peggy Walsh Craig, Steven Lopata, Nan McCarthy, Janet McConnaughey, R. W. Odlin, Robert Lee Riffle, Larry Sitton, Kit Snedaker, Dodie Stoneburner, and Maya Rushing Walker.

To the folks of the CompuServe Literary Forum's Children's Literature section for comments and critiques—to section leader Marsha Skrypuch, and to Merrill Cornish, Linda Grimes, and Rosemarie Riechel.

To Moses Orepesa, Jr., and D. J. Sieker for their comments on the manuscript.

To the martial artists of KoSho Karate in Tucson, who listened to these stories as I learned to tell them. To Rosina Lippi Green for her insights into the business of writing and her honesty and kind words.

And most especially to my husband, Gary, who has always believed in me.

Introduction

Most stories are either nonfiction or fiction, true or make-believe. But a legend is often both.

Most of the people in *Legends of the Martial Arts Masters* were real people. Tamo was a real monk who lived fifteen hundred years ago. Yet because he lived so long ago, we know almost nothing about what he was like as a person. The stories about what he could do have been told and retold so many times that we no longer know what is real and what is make-believe. On the other hand, Robert Trias died in 1989. Many of his students are still alive, still teaching karate, and still telling their students what they remember about Grandmaster Trias. But already Robert Trias is becoming a legend. Stories about him are told and retold, sometimes growing a little in the telling.

Did Ueshiba Osensei really disappear into thin air? Did Nai Khanom Tom really defeat twelve Burmese Bando fighters? Did Gogen Yamaguchi really fight a tiger? I don't know. That's the way I heard the stories, but maybe they had "grown" a little before I heard them.

Even if these aren't true in every detail, they are great legends. Why? Because legends aren't just about what happened. Legends are about how we feel when we hear stories about great people doing great things. Legends are about wondering whether people are really able to do such spectacular feats. Legends are about wondering if we could do great things, too.

*S*okon Matsumura was one of Okinawa's greatest martial artists. When he was a child, he studied Te, an Okinawan martial art. His Te teacher, Tode Sakugawa, noticed his courage and gave him the nickname Bushi, which means "warrior." As an adult Matsumura served the king of Okinawa by leading both the army and the king's personal bodyguards. He developed the Shuri-te style of karate to help him train the king's soldiers. Matsumura served the king of Okinawa so well that after many years, the king formally changed Matsumura's name to Bushi in recognition of his courage and service.

A Karate Master Fights a Bull

"Isn't he magnificent?" King Sho asked Matsumura. "He's too aggressive for most bull fights. He's already killed several other bulls in the arena."

Before them in a pen of the royal stables, a huge bull pawed at the ground. Its shoulder muscles, which were almost at Matsumura's eye level, strained as the powerful animal thrashed its head.

"Yes, your highness," Matsumura answered. "He is a magnificent beast."

"You will kill him," the king responded.

Matsumura was silent. He looked at the animal, the huge pointed horns, the massive head. The power. The majesty.

"Your highness?" he said, "I'm not sure what you are asking from me."

"At the festival tomorrow," the king said. "In the ring, at the festival. You will kill him with your bare hands. Everyone will see that the commander of my bodyguards, the great Matsumura, is the most powerful man in the land."

"Sir, I have never used my Te against an animal before. It's a defensive art, your majesty, not for slaughtering animals. Could I not serve you in another way?"

The king shot him a look of anger. "You presume to tell me how you should serve me? I bought this bull for you. I bought this bull to honor your skills as a martial artist before the festival. You will fight the bull. Do you understand?"

"Your Majesty . . ." Matsumura began.

"You will fight the bull, and you will win, or I will throw you into prison. Do you understand?"

"Yes, Your Majesty. I will fight the bull."

After sunset, Matsumura sat alone at the edge of the palace courtyard. He thought of the bull. It was a beautiful animal, strong and powerful. It would not be easy to break its neck, but he could do it. He could do it, but he did not want to.

"Use your Te only in defense," his teacher had taught him. "Use it to defend yourself, your family, your king, and your country. Use it to defend the defenseless innocent, but never provoke a fight. Never use your art simply to show off."

Killing a bull seemed like showing off to him. But he didn't want to go to prison. He began to walk the grounds. Perhaps the king would change his mind. No, that wasn't likely.

Matsumura walked through the garden, his mind on his problem. Absentmindedly he dragged his hand through the flower vines at the edge of the path. He felt their soft petals brush his fingers as he walked and thought. Suddenly a piercing pain shot through his hand. He jumped back. Out of his finger stuck a one-inch thorn from one of the king's Chinese flower bushes overhanging the path. Gingerly, Matsumura pulled the thorn from his finger. He tasted blood on his throbbing finger as he sucked the wound. It was amazing something so small could cause so much pain. Suddenly he had an idea. He dashed across the garden to the stables.

Pausing for a moment to straighten his uniform, he stepped through the stable door.

The workers jumped to their feet, surprised to see the captain of the guard, the great Matsumura, in the stables.

"I am the keeper of the stables," an older man said, as he stepped forward. "How may I serve you, sir?"

"Take me to the bull," Matsumura commanded. "I must look my adversary in the eye, learn his ways, if I am to fight him."

"Certainly, Lord Matsumura," the stable keeper motioned to a pen in the back of the stables. "After you, sir."

Matsumura walked to the pen, his eyes locked on the bull.

"Tie him," he commanded. "Tie him so he cannot move."

"Yes, sir." The stable keeper scrambled for two lengths of rope. One at a time, he looped them over the animal's head and tied them securely to the solid wood beams of the pen.

"Now leave," Matsumura commanded. "All of you leave."

The stable hands scrambled to the doors.

Matsumura climbed into the pen. The bull strained against the ropes. "The ropes don't seem very strong," Matsumura thought to himself. "If he breaks free, he'll trap me against the rails of the pen." The fear rose inside him, gripped his stomach like a hand, and twisted. Matsumura took a deep breath and faced the bull, faced his fear.

"The king says I must defeat you. But you are not my enemy." He reached up to his topknot, the tight bundle of hair he wore on top of his head. He pulled out a hairpin, and tested its point on his finger next to the thorn mark. A second tiny dot of blood rose. Matsumura had heard of martial arts masters who could kill with a hairpin. He hoped to save a life with one.

He assumed a sturdy fighting stance in front of the bull. The bull watched him curiously. "Forgive me, my friend," Matsumura said. Then from deep within his center, he let out a bloodcurdling shout, a kiai, and like lightning pricked the bull's nose with his hairpin.

The bull bellowed and strained against the ropes, his eyes wild. He thrashed his head tried to reach Matsumura with his horns. Matsumura watched the ropes. They held. Barely. Matsumura waited as calmly as he could. Eventually, the animal quieted. Again Matsumura let out a powerful kiai and again pricked the animal lightly with his pin. Again the bull struggled and tried to charge. Again Matsumura waited for the animal to stop struggling. Again, and again, and again—kiai, prick, kiai, prick. Several minutes later he walked out of the stables into the cool night air.

The next day at the festival, Matsumura, head of the king's bodyguards, walked around the edges of the arena. He checked the guards at the entrances, and posted an extra two in the back of the arena to watch for troublemakers. With his experienced eye, he scanned the crowd for anyone who might want to do the king harm. He saw none. The people of Okinawa were in a party mood. Colorful banners decorated the arena, and the smell of spicy roasted fish and other foods filled the air. These festivals were one of the high points of the year. The people loved the horseback-riding demonstrations, the fights, and the chance to eat and celebrate.

Matsumura made his way to the king's seat. He checked with the guards. All was well. As Matsumura turned to leave, the king noticed him and waved him over. Matsumura bowed deeply. Still munching the pear he had been snacking on, the king said, "I assume you are ready to meet the bull?"

"Of course, Your Majesty," Matsumura replied.

"I knew you would be," the king said, choosing a bunch of grapes from a bowl. "You have never disappointed me yet."

"I hope this won't be the first time," Matsumura thought to himself as he bowed and left the box. Disappointing a king was not good for one's health.

Matsumura heard his name called. He strode to the center of the arena amidst the cheers of the crowd. He felt the fear inside him rise. He took a deep breath and nudged the fear to the back of his mind. He wanted to meet the bull with his emotions and mind clear. He heard several dull thuds as the bull in its pen banged the rails with its shoulders. Matsumura watched it and wondered if his plan would work. If it didn't, he would be fighting for his life in a matter of moments.

He nodded to the stable keeper, who untied the rope holding the gate closed. The bull threw his weight against it and it popped open with a force that made the crowd gasp. Matsumura took a fighting stance. The bull spotted him and began moving forward. Matsumura waited. The bull picked up his speed to a trot. Matsumura waited. The bull bore down, almost upon him.

Quickly Matsumura shifted to let the bull pass. As he did, he shouted. Matsumura's kiai rang through the air like a shock wave. The crowd fell silent. The bull spun to look at Matsumura. For a moment time stood still. The crowd held its breath. The bull and Matsumura stood looking deep into each other's eyes. Matsumura kiaied again. A look of recognition crossed the bull's face. He turned and bolted for the far side of the arena. Matsumura followed. He kiaied. Again the bull ran.

Matsumura gave chase. The crowd broke into cheers. "Bushi! Bushi! Bushi!" they cried. "Warrior, warrior, warrior!"

The king finally stood. He raised a hand, and the crowd gradually fell silent.

"Matsumura," he shouted. "Come stand before me."

Matsumura backed away from the bull as the stable keeper and his assistants stepped out with ropes and prods to bring the animal back to his pen. He strode to the far side of the arena where the king stood and bowed deeply.

"Matsumura," the king said, "your power is great. Even the most powerful bull in the land does not dare do battle with you. From this day forward you will be known as 'Bushi Matsumura.' For you are indeed a great warrior."

Sumo is a traditional style of Japanese wrestling. Huge men, some of them weighing as much as 450 pounds, enter a packed-clay ring covered by a large roof that looks like a Shinto shrine. The ring is known as a dohyo, the wrestlers as rikishi. From a crouching position, the rikishi, wearing nothing but silk loincloths, crash into each other. To win the match, one of them has to tip the other over or push him out of the ring.

The Great Sumo Wave

Onami stood across from his opponent in the dohyo, the sumo ring. He estimated the opponent to be a good seventy-five pounds lighter than he. Size didn't guarantee him a victory, but it would certainly help. Onami looked into his opponent's eyes. They were cool, steady. Onami hoped his looked just as steady, but he doubted it. There was something about wrestling in a ring before a huge, cheering crowd that made him nervous.

Onami took a wide straddle stance, slowly rocked up on one foot, then dropped the other with a force he hoped would make the ground shake. Across the ring, his opponent was doing the same. Stamping the ground this way drove out any evil that may be lurking in the ring. Onami hoped it would also shake loose some of the growing fear rumbling in his belly. He picked up a handful of salt from a basket in the corner and scattered it in the ring, saying a quick prayer for safety. Then he moved to his side of the ring and squatted, arms stretched wide. The gyoji in charge of the match signaled with the colorful fan he held in his hand. The two wrestlers moved to the center and crouched, their knuckles in the sand that covered the clay ring.

Onami knew he had to win this match. He hadn't had a victory in a long time, a fact that caused him great shame among the wrestlers of his stable. "I can't lose this match," he told himself. "I can't lose. I have to win." His opponent charged, interrupting Onami's inner pep talk. Onami charged back. Quickly, almost automatically, he reached for the band around his opponent's waist. He felt it in his hand, but then his fingers slipped as his opponent shifted his weight. "I have to move," he thought as he felt his opponent's leg hook behind his own. He shifted ever so slightly, and that was all his opponent needed. Onami felt his feet go out from under him. A huge cheer went up for his opponent as Onami hit the hard clay of the ring.

"I don't know what the problem is," Onami said to his friend Takagawa the next day at practice. "I do fine here at the school. But when I get into the ring, I can be dumped by rikishi half my size."

"All you can do is keep working," his friend said. "It's only a bad case of jitters. If you practice hard enough, it's bound to go away sooner or later."

"I thought so, too," Onami said. "But that was over twenty losses ago. If I don't get a win soon, the Master is going to dismiss me from the stable."

"That kind of thinking is going to get you into trouble," Takagawa replied. "You can't do anything about yesterday or tomorrow. Let's just practice today."

The two friends squared off in the ring. Onami charged and easily pushed his friend from the circle. Other students climbed into the ring with him, and he pushed them out as well. Finally Onami's teacher stepped into the ring. Onami bowed low in respect. But when the opportunity presented itself, he twisted his teacher off balance and dumped him on the ground.

"Why can't I wrestle this well in the ring?" Onami muttered to himself as he returned to his room after practice. "Why can I defeat anyone, including my teacher, in training, but the moment I step into the ring, I can be defeated by any beginner who steps in with me?"

He hung is head in shame and puzzlement as he shuffled down the hall.

"Onami!"

Onami turned at the sound of his name. "Yes, teacher," he said.

"I want you to talk to someone who can help you with your wrestling," his teacher said. "Tomorrow morning you will present yourself at the Zen monastery. There you will ask for a man named Hakuju. Do what he tells you."

"Yes, teacher," Onami replied wondering what a man at a Zen monastery would know about sumo.

The sun had just barely poked above the horizon the next day when Onami knocked at the monastery gate. A young monk answered and took him to the temple where a thin old man sat in meditation. The young monk left, and Onami waited. The old man's body was still, silent. His face was a picture of complete relaxation. Yet despite the coolness of the morning air, perspiration ran freely down the old man's face. He was obviously engaged in some inner struggle Onami could neither see nor sense.

Eventually the old man opened his eyes, rose, and turned to Onami.

"You are Onami," he said.

"Yes," Onami replied bowing deeply.

"Your name means 'great wave.'"

"Yes."

"I hear you are not so great in the dohyo. I hear a tiny splash could push you over."

Onami cringed but said nothing.

"Would you like to become a great wave, pushing over everything in your path?"

"I would," Onami replied, "more than anything."

"Then kneel here," the old monk said, motioning to a small kneeling bench. "Close your eyes. Meditate. Picture a big wave."

Onami knelt, closed his eyes. In his mind he saw a wave, a large wave. It crashed on the beach before him. He wondered if he was becoming a better wrestler yet. He opened his eyes.

"I've seen the wave," he said rising to his feet. "What do I do next?"

"Next, you see the wave," Hakuju said motioning for him to kneel again. "I will be back this afternoon to check on you."

Onami knelt and closed his eyes again. In his mind he saw the wave. It rose and fell, rose and fell. Onami heard its thunder, saw it crash on the beach. All morning he watched the wave. And all morning he wondered how the wave was going to help him become a better wrestler.

That afternoon, Hakuju returned. "Have you been picturing a great wave?" he asked.

"Yes, sir," Onami replied.

"Tell me about it," Hakuju said.

"Well," Onami began, "it's large, and it's covered with foam, and it crashes on the beach." He paused, not sure what else to say.

"It sounds like a pretty small wave to me," Hakuju replied. "I told you to picture a big wave. I will be back at sunset to check on you."

Onami closed his eyes. The wave in his mind grew. It rose high above his head, crashed at his feet. Onami smelled the wind off the ocean, tasted the salt on his lips. The power of the wave shook the earth around him, filled him with its echo.

Onami was deep in his meditation when Hakuju returned that evening. "Tell me about the wave," he said.

Onami paused, not sure what to say. "It shakes the earth when it crashes. It's frightening, but it's also beautiful. It's more water than I have ever seen in my life," he said.

"It sounds like a pretty small wave to me," Hakuju replied. "I told you to picture a big wave. I will be back at sunrise to check on you."

Onami was disappointed. In a way, though, he was pleased to have more time to spend with the wave. He closed his eyes. All night the wave swelled and grew. Its sound was deafening inside Onami's mind. Suddenly, it leapt forward and picked up Onami from where he had been sitting on the beach. In its core, Onami rolled and tumbled until he came out the back of the wave. Sputtering water, Onami paddled to keep up, struggled to catch the wave, to become part of it. The wave picked him up and carried him, filled him with its power. It washed through the temple, carrying it away. It washed through Onami's school, carrying it away. It washed over the dohyo where Onami competed, carrying away the great roof and all Onami's competitors. Nothing could stand in the path of this great wave.

"Onami!" Hakuju's hand was on his shoulder. "Onami, it's morning."

Onami opened his eyes. Salt water rolled off his forehead. He blinked it back, surprised to see the temple still standing. The ground all around him was dry.

"Tell me about the wave," Hakuju said.

Onami broke into a huge grin. "I'm not sure I can," he said. "You should have been here. It was . . ." he paused, not sure how to describe the experience.

"Go home," Hakuju said. "And remember next time you step into the ring that you are Onami. You are the Great Wave."

Onami's opponent squatted opposite him beneath the great roof of the dohyo. Onami looked around. In his vision, the wave had carried all this away. "I am Onami," he said to himself. "I am the great wave."

The gyoji signaled with his fan. Onami felt the swell inside him. He crashed into his opponent, flowed over and through him, pushing him easily out of the ring. The judges gave the signal. He had won the match.

The 1964 Long Beach International Karate Championships is widely recognized as Bruce Lee's debut. Though he had appeared in twenty Hong Kong films before the age of 20, Long Beach brought him to the attention of Hollywood. Jay Sebring, a Hollywood hair stylist who cut the hair of several Hollywood stars, was at the tournament and watched Lee's demonstration. He talked up Lee's skills to his clients, eventually introducing Lee to Bill Dozier, the producer for "The Green Hornet." Lee's role as Kato, rocketed him to stardom, both in America and Hong Kong, where the program was called "The Kato Show." Before his untimely death in 1973, Lee taught celebrities, James Coburn, Steve McQueen, and Kareem Abdul-Jabbar to name a few. He also taught martial artists Dan Inosanto, Ted Wong, Taky Kimura, and Daniel Lee, who carried on his work teaching Jeet Kune Do.

Only grainy, silent fragments still exist of Bruce Lee's 1964 demonstration in Long Beach. This account, told by a fictional narrator, is based on those fragments, eyewitness accounts, and Lee's own words in interviews conducted in the early 1960s.

Introducing Bruce Lee

We were all pretty tough in those days. American martial artists in the 1950s and 1960s were mostly former servicemen who had fought in World War II and the Korean War. We all knew what it meant to be a fighter, and through hard experience, we had developed a deep respect for fighting systems that worked. The toughest, most skilled fighter, we believed, was king.

While in the service, some of us were posted in Asia, where we studied whatever Japanese and Korean martial arts were available to Americans. After we got out, we continue to practice any way we could. Some of us returned to Asia to study as civilians. Most of us went back to the States, found teachers, and picked up whatever we could wherever we could. The problem was that it was hard to get good instruction. Most traditional masters didn't want their martial art exposed to the masses, so only a few martial arts schools were open to the public, some in Hawaii, a couple in Arizona, some in California. I was in Illinois with a couple of other guys, sharing what we had learned in the service with each other, keeping an ear out for anyone, anywhere who could teach us another move, another form.

When word went out that Ed Parker was going to host a tournament in Long Beach, California, my buddies and I felt like we'd been invited to the biggest, best birthday party ever. We took time off work, threw our gis, the white uniforms of the Okinawan and Japanese arts, into our gym bags, and drove through the night. When we got there, we weren't disappointed.

The Long Beach Arena was a huge domed building surrounded by a grassy lawn. You could fit thousands of people into it without them bumping shoulders. Guys were practicing outside on the sunny lawn, trying techniques on each other. It was like Disneyland for karate guys. That's not even to mention the talent. Long Beach 1964 was the biggest collection of martial arts talent ever brought together in one place up to that time. Chuck Norris was there, and Superfoot Wallace. We saw Joe Lewis, Robert Trias, Jhoon Rhee, and Benny "The Jet" Urquidez—all the greats just walking around, talking, and sharing ideas. Altogether, 865 of us came to compete. Some were pretty poor, but others went on to become legends.

The best part, though, was the demonstrations. Takayuki Kubota broke a stack of bricks with his bare hands. These days that might not be unusual, but back then, we'd never seen anything like it. Jhoon Rhee demonstrated jumping kicks. He could do a jumping side kick to an opponent's head that was so high he was actually kicking down at the guy.

But perhaps the most impressive demonstration was from a fellow nobody had ever heard of. His name was Bruce Lee. He was 23 years old. When he started to speak he was a complete unknown. When he finished, everyone in the arena had an opinion about him, and everyone would remember his name.

It was August. The auditorium was hot, and the air conditioning wasn't working right. The organizers knew Lee wasn't going to be a very big draw, so they gave him a slot in the afternoon when everyone was groggy from lunch. I was nodding off from the heat. My buddy next to me was grouchy. We were lucky to catch the name when the MC announced Lee's demonstration.

"What's he wearing?" my buddy said as we applauded Lee's entry into the center of the arena. We were used to training in gis. Lee was wearing a black loose jacket and pants with elastic cuffs. "Looks like pajamas," my buddy commented.

"I doubt it's pajamas," I said. But I thought they lacked a bit of dignity as well. The fabric was floppy, and Lee didn't even wear a black belt.

Lee began to speak with his chin held high. He had an accent, but I could understand him just fine. He strutted a bit as he walked and talked. It looked like he was looking down his nose at the rest of us.

"Arrogant little so and so," my buddy whispered to me. I grinned back. I didn't mind arrogance. Where I came from, you could be as arrogant as you wanted so long as you could fight. If you couldn't fight, someone would be happy to cure you of your arrogance.

Lee was on the small side of average for an American martial artist, probably no more than 5'7" but I remembered the saying back when I was in the Marine Corps: "Marines come in two varieties: big and mean, and skinny and mean." Some of the toughest guys I'd fought with during the war were little, skinny guys. If this Lee fellow was tough, I had no problem with his size.

I watched as Lee began demonstrating something I'd never seen before. *Chi sao*, he called it, sticky hands. His opponent was trying to get in some kind of grab or strike or something, but Lee was stuck to him like glue, following the opponent's every move, tying his arms into knots. Every now and then, he would roll an arm off, and punch the guy in the face. It was different. I looked around. The guys I was sitting with were watching intently, but you could tell they weren't that impressed. Either that or they didn't like being lectured by this young guy with his nose in the air.

What impressed me, though, was the speed. The guy had the fastest hands I'd ever seen. He started his punch from wherever his hand was at the time. We were always taught to bring our power punches from as far back as possible. Lee started his punches sometimes inches from his opponent's face. There would be no way to block something that came in that fast from that close. But I wondered about the power. I figured Lee's punches would probably sting, but I doubted he could knock anyone down with them. Still, the speed was really impressive, and I wondered how I could learn that kind of speed myself.

Then Lee went into some wrist locks. From the very same position he'd used to stick to the fellow's punches, he began a lock that twisted his opponent's wrist and put him on the mat. You could see the audience beginning to warm up a bit at that. But the smiles didn't last long.

"The horse stance is useless as a fighting stance," Lee said. I was shocked. I could hear the gasps and murmurs through the auditorium. We practiced a lot of horse stances at my dojo. Everyone did. One of my favorite sparring stances was a horse stance, sideways to the opponent with my right side, my strong side back. It was a powerful stance, and I liked it. "The horse stance is all stability," Lee said. "But for many people, there is no mobility in it."

"The problem with traditional styles is all these fixed postures," Lee continued. "There is no room for individuality, no tailoring the technique to the body. So a fighter is forced to get into a horse stance even if he can't get out of it fast enough to fight." He did have a point. I'm a big guy, and though I liked my horse stances, I was always struggling with my speed. My speed and my knees. After a hard sparring match, my knees seemed to ache a lot more than the little guys' knees did.

"We are training cookie-cutter fighters," Lee said. "They are predictable, and they are slow, and they are weak because they are being forced to use movements that don't suit them."

That's when Lee threw the fastest kick I ever saw in my life. It came out of nowhere. It might have been a front kick, or maybe a round kick. I couldn't tell because it was in and out faster than my eye could follow.

"Wow," I said. It was almost a knee jerk reaction. I couldn't help but say it. "Wow." That's when I noticed that Lee threw the kick, and every other one of his techniques, from a very high stance. I knew in my gut I could never kick that fast out of my deep horse stance. Suddenly my whole world rearranged itself. All I wanted was to see what else this guy could do. All I wanted was to be able to do it, too.

I looked over at my buddy. He looked bored, maybe a bit ticked off. It surprised me he wasn't seeing how amazing this guy was.

"A kung fu man wants to be like water," Lee said. "Water is insubstantial. You can punch it all you want and never hurt it. It is soft, yet it can crash with great force and wear away rock, even granite. Water is soft and flexible. It adapts. We are training martial artists who are stiff and hard like rock. And when they get hit, they break. We should be training to be water."

Lee dismissed his partner. He talked a bit about fitness. It was, for once, something not too controversial among the karate players. He got down to do a push-up. It was no big deal. We did push-ups. Then he switched to a one-handed push-up. OK, that was a bit more impressive. But I could do a few on a good day. Then he picked up three of his fingers. I kid you not—he was doing a push-up on his thumb and index finger of one hand. I had no idea how he could do it, but I immediate saw the advantage. We did a lot of grabbing and poking. But we never trained finger strength like this. I itched to get back out to the lawn so I could try it.

"I could do that," my buddy said.

"Yeah," I said, "You say you *could*. But he just *did*. Guess which one I'm more impressed by."

Lee's time was almost up. I leaned forward, hoping to catch every nuance of the remaining demonstration. Another demonstration partner stepped out, a fellow in a gi and black belt. Lee took a relaxed stance in front of him, right foot forward. Someone came by and put a folding chair behind the fellow. Lee stood upright, a high stance that really wasn't much of a stance at all. He held out his right hand, his fingertips brushing his partner's chest. He shifted his weight and straightened his arm. His partner landed hard in the chair, which skidded back a foot or two before upending and dumping the fellow on the floor.

His partner looked stunned. He stood rubbing his chest, wincing when he breathed. I knew the feeling. I'd been hit like that before myself. But I'd never been hit like that from one inch.

"A karate punch," Lee explained, "is like an iron bar. Whack." He threw a punch any karate player would be proud to own. "But a kung fu punch is like an iron chain with an iron ball attached. It is relaxed, smooth, but when it lands, it hurts inside." Lee's partner, still rubbing his chest smiled ruefully and nodded.

Lee bowed to the audience, and that was it. Some of us applauded so hard our hands hurt. Others gave a few polite claps and rolled their eyes. Others looked angry as they crossed their arms across their chests. I couldn't believe we had all seen the same demonstration.

The MC announced a short break. My buddy and I decided to go outside and get some air. The breeze off the ocean was a welcome change from the stuffiness of the auditorium. My buddy headed immediately for the lawn, dropped down, planted his thumb and forefinger, and tried to do a push-up. He lost his balance and put down a knee.

"Almost," he said and tried again. His index finger collapsed. "Almost," he said again.

"Where did they say his school was?" I asked.

"Whose?" My buddy asked.

"Bruce Lee's," I said, puzzled. "Who did you think I meant? Where is his school?"

"Oakland," another fellow in a gi who was walking by said. "It's near San Francisco."

"Thanks," I said. "I guess that settles it then."

"What?" my buddy asked brushing grass from his knees.

"Oakland," I said. "I'm moving to Oakland."

*R*obert Trias is known as the "father of American karate." As a sailor in the United States Navy, he was the middleweight boxing champion for that branch of the service. During World War II, he was stationed in the British Solomon Islands in the South Pacific. There he studied karate and Hsing-I with Tung Gee Hsing, a Chinese martial artist. In 1945, he returned to the United States and opened America's first commercial karate school in Phoenix, Arizona. Later he became a highway patrolman in Arizona and is credited with adapting the tonfa, an Asian martial arts weapon, into the L-shaped police baton that law enforcement officers use today.

Robert Trias Finds a Teacher the Hard Way

Robert Trias popped his opponent with a quick jab to the chin, followed by another, and another. His opponent danced back, shook his head, and grinned. He moved in and shot an uppercut under Trias's lead arm but missed him by crucial inches. Trias slipped the punch and drove a glove into his opponent's ribs. The bell rang. The two men hugged each other, thumping each other's back with their bulky boxing gloves. They stepped through the ropes out of the ring.

"Geez, Robert," his opponent said, tugging at the laces of his glove with his teeth. "Every time I climb into the ring with you I come out feeling like a punching bag after a hard day."

"You got a few good ones in, too, Tom," Trias offered.

"Yeah, right. I think one was off your arm. And the other hit your shoulder, was it?"

Trias grinned, rolling his head from shoulder to shoulder. Boxing made him feel good. He took a swig of water from a bottle next to the ring.

"Serves me right for stepping into the ring with the Navy's top middleweight," Tom muttered, rubbing his jaw. "Every time I fight you I learn something, though. In another twenty years you'd better watch out!"

Trias ran a towel over his regulation Navy haircut. Even the spring in Solomon Islands was hot, and a lot more humid than his home in Arizona.

"Mr. Trias?"

Trias turned to see a small Asian man make his way to the ring. "I'm Robert Trias," he said.

"Pardon me for disturbing you. My name is Tung Gee Hsing. I understand you are a master of American box."

"Boxing," Trias said. "I've won my share of rounds."

"I myself am a student of Hsing-I, an ancient style of self-defense. I would like to teach you in exchange for lessons in American box . . . boxing."

"Thanks, but I do pretty well at defending myself already," Trias winked at Tom, who grinned back.

"Just so," Hsing replied. "That is why I would like to study with you."

"Thanks, but no thanks," Trias replied. "I have my Navy duties and my training. I really don't have time to take on a student. See you 'round, OK?"

"Yes. Yes, that will be fine," Hsing nodded, then turned to leave.

When he had gone, Trias turned to Tom. "Strange fellow. Ever heard of Hsing-I?"

"Nope," Tom replied. "But I've heard that some of those Chinese boxers fight like tigers."

The next afternoon, Trias was skipping rope in the gym when the door opened and Tung Gee Hsing entered. Hsing took a seat on a bench in the corner and watched quietly. Trias put away the jump rope and began working out on the heavy bag. Dust puffed from the stitching with each blow. Somehow, though, his timing was off. Trias felt Hsing's eyes heavy on his back. It made him nervous. Finally, he turned and walked to the bench. Hsing stood.

"Are you here to ask for boxing lessons again?" he asked.

"Yes," Hsing replied. "And to offer to teach you Hsing-I."

"I told you I'm not interested."

"Yes, you did."

"Then why don't you just leave?"

Hsing bowed and left.

The next afternoon, when Trias entered the gym, there was Hsing waiting for him. He bowed to Trias and smiled.

"You don't take a hint, do you?" Trias commented as he dropped his gear on the bench next to Hsing. Hsing just smiled. "Maybe the direct approach will work. What will it take to get you to leave me alone?"

"Would you like to fight?" Hsing asked.

"Me? Fight you? No offense, but you're hardly in my weight class. You'd be at a disadvantage."

"It's fine. Hsing-I doesn't use weight classes."

Trias shook his head. "If I beat you, will you leave me alone?"

"Certainly," Hsing replied.

"Then let's find you some gloves," Trias smiled.

"Thank you, but that really won't be necessary. Unless you would prefer . . ."

"It makes no difference to me either," Trias replied. "But why don't you put them on anyway. They'll protect your hands. Tom," he called out to his training buddy, "Call the guys outside, would you? They might want to see this. It looks like we've got a match between me and our persistent friend here."

Trias danced around his opponent, sizing him up. Hsing stood steady but light on his feet, shifting stance ever so slightly to adjust for Trias's position. Trias jabbed; Hsing slipped it. He jabbed again; Hsing dropped under the punch and tagged Trias's ribs.

Trias's eyes grew wide. The punch didn't look like much, but the force rattled through him. He drew a fast, deep breath and looked at his opponent. Not a hint of satisfaction, not a hint of any emotion crossed his calm face. OK, so it was going to take more than jabs to get this guy's attention.

One, two, three. Trias sent in a volley of punches. One, two, three, four. Hsing was blocking and slipping some of his best combinations. The punches that did land seemed to be swallowed up by his body without hurting him at all. So the guy was good. But could he last? Trias picked up the intensity. Try as he might, he could not land a thing. Finally in desperation he set up a punch to the jaw that would blast through any defense. One, two, three, four, blast. The punch flew in like a bullet, and landed on thin air.

Trias caught his balance in time to see Hsing's glove completely fill his field of vision. Another punch caught him in the gut, and another on the side of the head. His feet went out from under him.

Trias's vision cleared, and he saw Hsing's hand extended. He grasped it and pulled himself up. Trias looked at the small man as he stepped through the ropes and left the ring. He had never seen a combination like that. He'd never seen anyone who could evade punches like that. Frankly, he'd never seen a man fight like that. Silently Trias left the ring.

Hsing was in the corner removing his gloves. Trias pulled off his right glove and walked over. He extended his hand. "Mr. Hsing," he said, "Will you teach me?"

"*The Three Sons*" *is a traditional legend. No one is sure where it originated or whether it is a true story. People in many countries and from many cultures tell it.*

The Three Sons and the Sword Master

Once there was a great sword master. Among his pupils were his three sons. The sons were proud of their father and enjoyed studying with him. They put in long, hard hours mastering his art.

One day an old friend and training partner from the master's younger years came to visit. He too was known throughout the land as a great sword master. The two men sat together in the master's front room, drinking tea and telling stories.

"My friend," said the guest to the master, "I would like very much to meet your three sons and to have them show me how they have progressed in the way of the sword."

"Certainly," said the master. "I will call them."

The master walked to a mantel where several large, heavy vases stood. He took one of the vases from its place and balanced it on top of the door so it would fall when the door opened. He then called the name of one of his sons.

"In a minute, Father," the son called back from the garden, where he was practicing with his sword. He was in the middle of a difficult move. With a few more tries he would get it right. Five minutes later he looked up from his practice and remembered that his father wanted him. Sheathing his sword, he dashed through the house.

The two men waited in the front room. They saw the knob of the door turn quickly and the door fly open. The vase on top of the door fell and hit the son squarely on top of his head. The son let out a roar and drew his sword. Before the vase even hit the floor, he had sliced through it, shattering it into a hundred pieces. Only then did he see that his "attacker" had been one of his father's vases. He sheathed his sword, smiled sheepishly, bowed to his father and his guest, and began cleaning up the pieces of the vase.

"He is fast," the guest said.

"Yes, and strong," the father replied.

"Do you think that someday he could become adept with a sword?"

"Yes," the father said smiling at his son, motioning for him to sit and join them for tea. "Someday, perhaps."

The three sat together talking for a few minutes before the father rose, took a second vase from the mantel, and balanced it over the door. He called the name of his second son.

"Yes, Father," the second son called from the garden, where he had been practicing with a few friends. "Excuse me, guys," he said, bowing to the students he had been practicing with. Then he sheathed his sword and walked down the hallway to the front room.

The master, the guest, and the first son saw the knob turn and the door open. The vase fell from its place. The second son spun out of the way, his hand on the hilt of his sword and ready to draw. Only then did he see that it was his father's vase that had fallen. He dove and caught it before it hit the ground. The vase still in his arms, he bowed to his father and his guest. He then walked over to the mantel and replaced the vase exactly where his father always kept it.

"He has very good reflexes," the guest said.

"Yes, and a good memory. He has developed most of the essential skills," the father replied.

"Do you think that someday he could become adept with a sword?"

"Yes," the father said smiling at his son, motioning for him sit and join them for tea. "Someday, perhaps."

The four sat together for a few minutes. Again the father rose, took a vase from the mantel, and placed it atop the door. He called the name of his third son.

His third son was in the garden practicing cuts with his sword. His blade sliced easily through the practice mats he had prepared for the purpose. When he heard his father's voice, he stopped his practice, carefully wiped his sword, sheathed it, and walked to the front room.

The master, the guest, and the two sons saw the doorknob turn slightly, then pause. For a few seconds there was no movement in the door at all. Then slowly it opened. The third son's hand appeared over the top. Carefully holding the vase in place, he pivoted gracefully under it into the room. He closed the door without ever having moved the vase.

"You must be proud," the guest said to the master.

The master nodded.

"Well," said the guest after the five of them had sat and talked for several hours, "I must go." He motioned to the first son to come to him. The son knelt before him and bowed deeply. "My boy," the guest said, handing him a fine watch. "Always be aware of where you are at any given time. A person must master his own awareness before mastering any art."

He then motioned to the second son, who knelt before him and bowed. The guest handed him a fine handmade book. The son paged through it to see that each of the beautifully crafted pages was empty. "My boy," he said, "a collection of finely honed skills is like a blank book. The pages of your life as a martial artist are now ready for you to write whatever you wish in them. Write well."

He then motioned to the third son, who knelt before him and bowed. The guest handed him a small piece of jewelry, a simple pin with a small diamond in the center. The guest looked into the son's eyes as he handed him the pin. The son looked back and smiled with understanding. Neither said a word.

The master walked to the front gate with his guest. The two bowed with a lifetime's respect for each other. The guest turned and walked out the gate into the city.

Krav Maga is the martial art of the Israeli Defense Force. Today, it is a practical, effective self defense style studied by soldiers and civilians worldwide. But before Krav Maga's techniques ever reached Israel, before they became the style they are today, they were refined and honed on the streets of Nazi-occupied Slovakia.

How Imi Lichtenfeld Lived to Invent Krav Maga

Imi Lichtenfeld glanced up at the Betar sentry atop a nearby apartment building. The first signal was out. A bed sheet hung from the chimney signaled that the attackers were inside the perimeter. When the sentry took the sheet off the chimney and began to wave it, Imi's younger guards would begin to rain bricks and garbage down from the rooftop. Then the older guards, the fellows in their late teens and twenties like Imi, would fall on the enemy and make them think twice about crossing the perimeter again.

Imi shifted his weight back and forth from foot to foot. He was nervous; he didn't mind admitting that. It wasn't that he lacked fighting skills. In fact, he was probably the best fighter in either the Betar (the local Jewish Nationalist youth organization) or his own guards. In 1928 alone, Imi had won the Slovak National wrestling, boxing, and gymnastic titles. His father, who was also his jujitsu teacher, had taught him how to defend himself.

No, Imi didn't question his skills. What he questioned was what his attackers would be bringing to the fight. This was no wrestling match. This could become a fight to the death. Imi, a Jewish man living in Nazi-occupied Bratislava, Slovakia, knew the dangers all too well. His attackers were Hitler Youth, young men who believed in driving all the Slovakian Jews from the country no matter the cost.

Already these young Nazi wannabes had roamed the streets of the Jewish sector breaking windows and robbing and vandalizing shops and homes. They humiliated the Jewish elders, and beat the young men and boys. The things they said to the girls and women made Imi's blood boil. All of the Hitler Youth trained in hand-to-hand combat. Some had weapons. A few wouldn't hesitate to use them. Killing a Jew in Slovakia wasn't considered to be much of a crime. On the other hand, if Imi had to use deadly force, the authorities would "disappear" him overnight.

None of that was relevant, he told himself, waiting for the signal to begin. His people were in danger, and he must fight to defend them. It was in his blood to protect the defenseless. So he and a bunch of his wrestling and boxing buddies crouched behind a wall waiting to engage. Across the street, the Betar boys formed the other half of a pincer movement. All eyes were on the lookout on the roof.

The flag went up, and Imi heard the crash of bricks, rocks, and broken glass as it rained from above. The Nazis cried out and swore.

"Now," he shouted. He charged into the melee and grabbed the closest attacker he could. He pulled him into a knee and dropped him to the pavement. The next fellow he dropped with an elbow. He looked around for a third. That's when he felt it, a searing pain in his upper arm. He looked down. The sleeve was sliced open. He turned to face a big fellow in a light brown shirt and black shorts, holding an eight-inch knife like someone who knew how to use it. Imi barely had time to react. The attacker swung the knife in a narrow arc. Imi threw up his arms and blocked the arm. He latched on to it with both hands like his life depended on it. The attacker pulled back, and Imi went with him. He swung his other arm at Imi's head, but he wasn't much of a puncher, and Imi was able to evade most of the impact.

"What now?" he thought. If he let go with one hand to try to get in a strike, he would almost certainly lose control of the knife. But clinging to the arm, he was as trapped as the attacker. He lifted a foot and stomped into the attacker's instep. He lifted a knee and tried to drive it into the groin, but the angle was all wrong. He shoved, but the attacker's balance was too good. That's when he saw someone with a trash can come running through the melee. Imi let go of the arm and watched as a buddy brought the big can down on the attacker's head. Imi nodded his thanks and looked for someone else to engage.

It didn't take long for the Hitler Youth to begin to fall back. Imi saw blood staining brown shirts and rips and stains in the jackets of thugs who didn't wear the uniform but just came along for the fight.

"Pride!" The Betar boys shouted. They dusted off their uniforms and assessed their wounds, knowing before even looking that they would be willing to suffer much worse to protect their people.

Imi checked the sleeve of his shirt. The shirt was ruined, but Imi, who had little interest in fancy uniforms, had worn an old shirt to the fight. He opened the slit a little wider. The cut in his arm bled freely but wasn't deep. Imi breathed a sigh of relief. Hospitals, like most Slovak and German-run businesses, were no longer open to Jews. Maybe he would see if his mother could put in a few stitches with her sewing thread.

"Arm still attached?" Alex Citron, leader of the Betar asked, slapping him playfully on the other shoulder.

"A scratch," Imi replied.

"We did well," Alex commented. "The plan went off just as we planned it."

"Mm," Imi replied. His fight nagged at him. He kept running it through his mind. If he hadn't been rescued by a trashcan, he might still be attached to that boy's arm. "Do you have some time tomorrow?" he asked Alex.

"I think so," Alex replied. "What do you need?"

"I need you to try to stab me," Imi said.

The next afternoon Imi showed Alex the kind of stab the Hitler Youth had used. Alex grabbed the chunk of wood they were using instead of a knife and came in fast. Imi threw up both arms and grabbed. It was almost instinctive. But here he was again, stuck in a defensive position.

"Do it again," he said. He blocked with a single hand and grabbed the knife hand. Alex wrenched the hand free and stabbed.

"Do it again," Imi said. Again, Imi grabbed, and again Alex twisted free and stabbed.

That's when it dawned on Imi; the problem was not the knife itself. The problem was the knife in the hands of a conscious attacker. "Do it again, slower this time," he said.

Alex came in at half speed. Imi slipped the attack, grabbed the knife hand with his left hand and at the very same moment thrust his right palm heel into Alex's chin. Alex's head rocked back and he closed his eyes trying to keep Imi's fingers out of them. Despite the slowness of the movement, Alex stumbled backward a little. Imi grabbed his wrist and twisted, kicking Alex's feet out from under him.

"Do it again," Imi said, and repeated the movement. They tried the movement several times slowly, then picked up the speed. Then they tried it with the knife coming in from another angle.

"That's it," Imi said. "It's not defend, pause, attack. It's defend with an attack. Both. Simultaneously." He put his hand out and took the stick from Alex. "Your turn," he said.

The Hitler Youth attacks came erratically. Some weeks there would be none. Other weeks there would be one almost every day. Imi's guards and Alex's Betars patrolled the perimeter, sending runners if more defenders were needed. Imi taught fighting techniques to anyone who wanted to learn. Each time he fought the Nazi youth, he would make a mental note of what worked and what didn't. Street fighting was very different from wrestling, different even from boxing and jujitsu. Imi learned to be fast, stable, powerful and accurate in finding soft, vulnerable points on his attacker. Everything he learned he taught to anyone wanted to practice with him.

One day after practice, Alex took him aside.

"I talked to Zolli this morning," he said. "You know he has friends on the police force."

"I'm not sure how friendly Zolli's 'friends' are," Imi replied, packing his boxing gloves into a bag. "They do work for the Nazis after all."

"They're friendly enough to save your life," Alex replied. Imi looked up from his bag, his full attention suddenly on Alex. "Zolli's friend says the police department knows you've been teaching us to fight. And they know that you're behind a lot of the broken bones the Hitler Youth are coming home with. Zolli says your file at the police office is quite detailed, and last week it was marked "SB.""

"SB?" Imi asked.

"SB stands for the German term for 'special handling,'" Alex replied.

"I assume that doesn't mean they're going to treat me to a night on the town," Imi said quietly.

"They're going to kill you," Alex said bluntly.

Imi sat down on the bench along the gym wall. Alex sat next to him. "What I'm going to tell you is not common knowledge," Alex said. "Betar has arranged for a ship. It will come up the Danube River and pick up as many Jews as we can carry. We're going to Palestine."

"I'm not Betar," Imi said, "and I've told you I really don't want to join."

"That's OK," Alex said. "I've talked to the rest of the leadership, and they all want you and your family to come with us."

To call the *Pencho* a ship was generous. It was a creaky wooden paddle boat, 165 feet long and 40 feet wide, that had been hauling live-stock and coal up and down the Danube River for decades. It had a flat bottom and a mere five-foot draft, making it better suited to river travel than the open water of the Mediterranean. But Zolli planned to sail it down the Danube, onto first the Black Sea and then the Aegean Sea, and then across the Mediterranean to Palestine.

Imi and Zolli went down the ladder to the hold. Washrooms and toilets had been built down the center of a long room. Along the sides of the ship were shelves.

"What goes on those shelves?" Imi asked.

"You do," Zolli replied with a grin. "Those are bunks."

"They're no more than five feet long," Imi exclaimed.

"Five feet, three inches," Zolli said. "Two and a half feet wide, two feet of headroom."

Imi shook his head. "Why so small?" he finally asked.

Zolli sighed. "The Nazis are killing us," he replied. "They used to be content with robbing us and kicking us out of the country. But now they're killing us. The Aliyah Bet organization that's bringing us into Palestine, is hearing stories from other refugees. It started with 'trouble makers.' But now, one by one, our leaders are being arrested, taken away, and then never seen again."

"That's what you think will happen to me," Imi said. Zolli nodded.

"Our contacts in Palestine think they won't stop with just the lead-ers. They think they will start killing all of us soon. If they are right, I will inconvenience a few people to pack more of us in."

"How many?" Imi asked.

"300," Zolli replied.

Imi whistled softly. "I have my doubts," he said. "Do you think this tub will hold that many?"

"It will hold what it has to hold," Zolli replied.

The *Pencho* sailed from Bratislava in May of 1940 carrying 514 passengers. All the way down the river, Imi and the others were harassed, delayed, and extorted. In October they finally motored out onto the Aegean Sea. Wind and high seas nearly capsized the shallow river boat. Within days, the boiler exploded, and the ship was wrecked on the rocks of Kamilanisi, a tiny uninhabited island. Food and water were short, and the *Pencho* carried only one lifeboat.

Imi and four others volunteered to take the lifeboat and row for help. The island of Crete was forty miles to the south. With four strong rowers and a man on the tiller, they could row around the clock and make landfall in thirty hours, maybe less if the winds were with them.

The winds were not with them. When they were halfway to Crete, a storm blew in. The sea began to roll and crash with waves so high they looked like walls of water. Rain and spray soaked them to the skin. They rowed with all their strength just to keep the boat pointed the right direction. Finally, they saw the lights of the harbor. Exhausted, hands bleeding, muscles nearly empty, they fought the current, gaining only inches with each stroke. That's when one of the oars snapped. No matter how hard they pulled, they couldn't fight the current with only three oars. In exhaustion and despair, they fell into the bottom of the boat and slept while the wind and water pulled them out into the Mediterranean.

On the fourth day, the food and water were long gone. The rain had started again. The boat was taking on water. Imi had an ear infection and a high fever and was in and out of consciousness. He knew he would almost certainly die—all of them would die. The little boat would be swallowed up by the water of the Mediterranean, and nobody would know about the *Pencho* passengers still marooned on a barren island.

They were almost out of hope when they heard one of the finest sounds they had ever heard in their lives. An engine. It was a British scout plane.

A British destroyer picked up the five refugees. Grateful to be alive, they told the commanding officer about the *Pencho*, and begged him to radio for help. They were safe. And soon the *Pencho* would be safe. Or so they thought. The next day, Italian submarines and aircraft found the destroyer and opened fire on it. Imi awoke from his fevered sleep to the sounds of explosions. The British sailors fought off attack after attack on their way to Alexandria. There they dropped Imi and his four companions in a POW camp until they could prove they were Czech, not German. After extensive interviews and interrogations—and more requests to know the status of the *Pencho*—the British finally released the men. Imi went immediately to a hospital. His infected ear required three surgeries. The doctor said a weaker man would not have survived.

Meanwhile, the British had ignored the pleas to look into the fate of the *Pencho* passengers. Eventually, the Italian navy picked them up, and placed them in an internment camp for the rest of the war. They were not free, but they were grateful. News was filtering throughout Europe about mass deportations of Jews, about family members disappearing never to be heard from again.

That is why when Imi had recovered from his surgeries, he didn't immediately head for either Italy or Palestine. Rather he signed on with the Free Czechoslovak Legion, which was fighting Germany in North Africa under the command of the British Army. The sooner Germany was defeated, the sooner they could be chased out of Slovakia. Imi knew his people wouldn't be safe as long as the Nazis continued to occupy their country.

Imi gained a reputation as a fierce fighter, a reputation that made its way all the way to Palestine and the Haganah, the Jewish military organization in Palestine. In 1944, they offered him the chance to live in Palestine and train fighters. Imi jumped at the chance.

Imi stood in front of a group of young Haganah, men and women who grew up in Palestine as well as others who had come from countries all over Europe fleeing the Nazis. They would soon be protecting the Jewish population of Palestine, just as he did when he was their age.

"The fighting style you are about to learn is called Krav Maga," Imi told his students "There is one thing you need to understand about fighting. A real fight is not like a boxing match or a wrestling match. Real life is about doing whatever you need to do to survive and prevail. If you do not survive, who will protect our people? Now let me show you what I learned fighting Hitler Youth on the streets of Bratislava and Nazi soldiers in North Africa."

In September of 1943, when the Allies liberated the camp where the *Pencho* passengers were held, almost all of the 514 passengers were still alive. In June of 1944, most of them sailed again for Palestine, this time in an ocean liner. The Slovakian Jews who remained in Slovakia, the people Imi had fought to defend, were not so fortunate. By October of 1942, two-thirds of the Jewish population of Slovakia had been sent to death camps. Of the nearly 89,000 Jews in Slovakia before the war, only around three hundred of those who stayed in the country survived.

In 1948, the land that had been previously known as Palestine became the State of Israel. The Haganah was folded into the Israeli Defense Force. Imi became Chief Instructor for Physical Fitness and Krav Maga at the IDF School of Combat Fitness. He continued to refine and improve Krav Maga. Today it is practiced around the world by soldiers and civilians, Jews and Gentiles.

*T*sukahara Bokuden was a master of the sword. According to legend, he was never once defeated in a sword fight in his life. As a rich Japanese nobleman, Bokuden didn't hold a regular job, but traveled the countryside looking for adventure and chances to do good. He also taught students. One of the things he is remembered for is developing the bokken, a wooden practice sword still used today. The bokken gave his students the opportunity to practice without getting cut by a live sword.

The Sword Style of No Sword

Bokuden learned back against a pile of rice sacks. It was a beautiful, warm, summer day, a perfect day for a boat ride. He looked around at the other passengers on the ferry that was taking him across the lake. A young mother clutched at the belt of her five-year-old as he leaned over the side, dragging his hand in the water. An old woman sat properly upon a keg near the gangplank, her parcels at her feet. In the bow of the boat a scruffy-looking young samurai was talking to an older man.

"Then I cut him down with a single stroke," the young samurai boasted.

"Why?" asked the old man.

"Because he looked like he wanted to challenge me," the samurai said. "Nobody challenges me and lives."

"Um-hum," said the old man turning to survey the scenery.

"Are you questioning what I'm saying?" the young samurai snapped.

"I'm just looking at the scenery," the old man replied.

"You sound like you're challenging what I'm saying," the samurai said, standing.

"Sir," the old man replied, "I am old. I have no weapons. Even if I didn't believe you, why would I challenge you? It doesn't matter to me how good you are. Whether you are the greatest swordsman in the country or just some guy with a blade, you are obviously better than I am. That's all that matters, and I am quite willing to admit that."

"Are you mocking me?" the samurai shouted, his hand on the hilt of his sword. "I'm not just 'some guy with a blade.' I am the greatest swordsman in the country."

"I am," he said to the young mother, who was watching him with fearful eyes. Then he turned to the old woman. "I am!"

Bokuden cleared his throat loudly. The samurai spun around and for the first time noticed him lying back against the rice sacks. The samurai's eyes looked Bokuden up and down and came to rest on the two swords Bokuden wore on his belt.

"My name is Tsukahara Bokuden," Bokuden said, hoping his reputation as a sword master would be enough to quiet the loudmouth.

"Never heard of you," the young samurai replied. "What style of sword art do you practice?"

"The style of no sword," Bokuden answered continuing to relax against the sacks. "It's very popular. I'm sure you as a great swordsman have heard of it."

"The style of no sword?" the samurai replied. "That's ridiculous. There's no such style!"

"Sure there is," Bokuden said. "It's the style that says that a swordsman's skill isn't measured by how many men he's killed. A swordsman's skill is measured by how many fights he can walk away from undefeated."

The young samurai looked puzzled.

"It may be a bit difficult for you to understand," Bokuden said. "No matter. All you need to know is that it's the style that will allow me to put an end to your foolish bragging without ever drawing my sword."

The young samurai took a step back, almost tripping over the old woman's parcels. He pulled his sword halfway out of the scabbard.

Bokuden held out a hand. "Not here, my foolish, young adversary," he said. "We don't want to injure any of these good people." He scanned the lake, then called to the rower who was rowing them across. "I hate to inconvenience you sir," he said, "but could you row us over to that island over there?" Bokuden motioned toward a small rocky island. "If you'll just pull alongside those rocks, I can take care of this problem quickly. It won't take long. I promise." The rower nodded. The young samurai glared.

"Nobody insults me like that and lives to tell about it," he hissed at Bokuden.

Bokuden smiled back. "Patience," he said.

The rower pulled alongside a large rock. The young samurai pushed his way past the old woman and scrambled ashore.

"What are you waiting for?" he shouted to Bokuden, his hand on the hilt of his sword.

"Just a moment," Bokuden replied. "Remember, mine is the style of no sword." He pulled first his wakizashi, his short sword, from his belt. He handed it in its sheath to the rower, who shifted his oar to his other hand to take it. He then removed his katana, his long sword, and handed that too to the rower. The rower set down his oar and took it.

"Now," Bokuden said, "watch carefully, and you will see the swiftness and efficiency of the style of no sword." He picked up the oar and pushed the boat away from the rock where the young samurai stood. He rowed the ferry out a few hundred feet, handed the oar back to the rower, and collected his swords.

Walking back to his rice sacks amidst the ever-fainter shouts of the samurai still on the island, Bokuden thought what a nice day it was for a boat ride.

Yasutsune "Ankoh" Itosu was an Okinawan martial artist. He worked as a secretary to the king of Okinawa and studied karate under Sokon Matsumura, the head of the king's bodyguards. When a new Okinawan public school system was opened, Itosu suggested that karate be taught as a part of physical education classes. He believed that young students who study karate learn not only how to defend themselves but also how to stay healthy and live peacefully in society. In 1901, he became the first teacher to teach karate in the schools.

Itosu was an average-sized man. He didn't look like an athlete, but had a muscular chest and arms and legs that were much stronger than they looked. He was known for his ability to take a punch and for his powerful hands that could crush a green bamboo stalk.

A Karate Master Changes a Bully's Ways

The bully was young and strong the day he picked a fight with Ankoh Itosu. Despite that strength, the fight was the stupidest (and last) street fight of his life.

As bullies often do, Kojo thought he was toughest guy in town. He practiced fighting with a group of young men every evening after work. Each evening they practiced techniques with one another, and then each weekend they went downtown to the waterfront district in Naha, the local port city. There they'd find sailors, dockworkers, and laborers who had come to town for a good time. Some of them would be drinking too much. None of them would need much of a nudge to fight. Kojo and his friends would pick a fight and try out their newest techniques. Sometimes they'd win. Sometimes they'd lose. Each time they'd take what they learned home, work on it to make it more effective, then go back to town the next weekend to try it out again.

The first time Kojo saw Ankoh Itosu was one of those weekends. He and his friends had gone down to the waterfront to meet a ship that had just come in. An old man was standing on the dock talking to one of the sailors.

"If you want a challenge, try him," Kojo's friend said to him, pointing to the old man.

"Why?" Kojo asked. "He doesn't look so tough to me."

"That's Itosu," his friend said.

"Itosu the karate master?" Kojo could hardly believe his ears. The man had a long gray beard and deep wrinkles in the corners of his eyes. He was at least thirty years older than the oldest of Kojo's gang, and he was several inches shorter and several pounds lighter than Kojo himself. "He doesn't look so tough," Kojo said.

"Try him," the friend said, a dare in his eyes.

"It would be good for bragging rights," Kojo thought, for at that time he was still thinking like a bully. "I could say that I beat the great Ankoh Itosu. Even if I couldn't beat him, if I could just get one good punch in on him, it would make me respected, admired among my friends." The bully watched Itosu point to a nearby restaurant and bow to the person he had been talking to.

"Wait over there," Kojo said to his friends, motioning to a spot across the street. "Watch closely. You may learn something." They grinned and trotted off.

The bully figured that his best bet was to catch Itosu by surprise. He walked quietly around the corner of the restaurant, flattened himself against the front of the building, waited for Itosu to come around to the entrance. Soon he heard footsteps on the gravel. Itosu was going to walk right past Kojo's corner. Kojo rubbed his knuckles and smiled to himself.

Itosu rounded the corner. Without warning, the bully sprang out from the shadows. With a loud cry, he wound up and threw his best punch. Itosu's head snapped around as he saw the punch coming. But rather than block he just let out a noise that sounded a little like "Ummph." The bully had his full weight behind the punch and landed it on Itosu's ribs just in front of his left arm. It landed hard, but simply bounced off. With a movement so quick he didn't even see it, Itosu grabbed the bully's punching hand and tucked it under his left arm. The pain shot up the bully's arm like a lightning bolt.

"And who might you be?" Itosu asked.

"I'm—I'm Kojo," the bully replied, gasping for breath against the pain. "Actually, Kojiro. My friends call me Kojo." His friends. Where were his friends? Out of the corner of his eye, he saw them across the

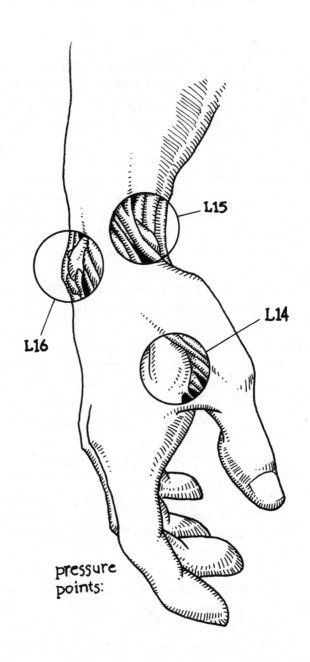

L15

L16

L14

pressure
points:

street watching everything. They made no move to come to Kojo's rescue.

"Well, Kojo," Itosu said, "why don't you join me? I think we have a few things to talk about."

Kojo was in no position to say no. Itosu had his arm tucked under his. He tweaked the wrist every now and then just to let the young man know who was in charge. Yet most of the persuasion came from his grip. Kojo felt like his hand was in a vise. It throbbed to the beat of his pulse.

The two of them, Itosu and the bully, walked into the restaurant like that, to all appearances two good friends walking arm in arm. Itosu pulled up two chairs with his other hand, and they sat, the bully's hand still in the vise. His fingers were going numb.

"So, Kojo," Itosu said as the server brought sake and two cups, "do I know you? Why is it you felt that you needed to attack me?" He sipped his sake casually with his unoccupied arm.

"Well, sir," Kojo said, "it was a dare. My friends dared me. And I thought . . ." He paused. Given a few moments to reflect, he wasn't really sure what he had been thinking.

"I see," Itosu replied. "Your friends were the young men I saw across the street?"

He'd seen them! It was pretty clear that Itosu didn't miss much.

"Yes," Kojo said. "Sometimes we come into town, go down to the docks or to the restaurant district. We, um, we fight, sir. We practice our karate." Kojo suddenly realized how silly that sounded.

"I see," Itosu said. He tweaked Kojo's wrist again as he reached to refill his sake cup. The pain streaked from the wrist up through the elbow to the shoulder. "And what does your karate teacher say about this?"

"Well," Kojo said through gritted teeth, "We don't really have one."

"Ah," Itosu said with a big smile. "So that's the problem." He released Kojo's arm. The young man rubbed his hand trying to erase the dents Itosu's finger had made. The hand throbbed and prickled as the blood returned to the fingers. Itosu filled a sake cup and pushed it toward his companion. "What you need is a teacher. You will study with me."

"Sir?" Kojo replied. "Study with you, sir?"

"That's what I said, isn't it?" Itosu finished his second cup of sake and pushed it and the pitcher away. "We need to work on your speed and your kiai. Your punch isn't too bad, but you'll have to relearn your hip movement to make it stronger. And of course, you'll have to stop fighting down by the docks."

"Yes, sir," Kojo said.

"And you will have to stop trying to frighten old men." Itosu grinned at the young man gingerly grasping a sake cup with his reddened hand. "You never know," Itosu said, "when you do that sort of thing, someone could get hurt."

Traditional Chinese Opera is a form of live musical theater that goes back to the earliest days of China. To act out stories of historic battles, Chinese opera players had to be spectacular acrobats and martial artists. Most of them began training as children in schools that taught them all the skills they would need to enact thrilling battle scenes on stage. This is the story of the most famous Chinese opera player of them all.

The Legend of Kong-sang (Jackie) Chan, Master Acrobat of the Chinese Opera

Seven-year-old Kong-sang wasn't sure why his parents had taken him to the Chinese Opera Research Institute, but he had his suspicions.

Maybe it was because he could never seem to sit still. It wasn't that he didn't try. He was a good son who wanted to make his family proud. But no matter how hard he tried, some part of him always seemed to be in motion. He'd get his hands to stop fiddling with something only to find that his leg was twitching up and down, almost as though it had a mind of its own. He was never happier than when he was running full speed through the back alleys of Hong Kong or even through his family's small house. His mother called him Cannonball. She said it with a smile, but she also called him that when his charging through the house broke things. Maybe his parents brought him to the institute because they didn't want to live with a cannonball anymore.

Or maybe he was there was because of his grades. Kong-sang wasn't much of a student. It wasn't that he didn't try. He studied as hard as he could to make his parents proud of him. But something was wrong. When other student looked at the characters that made up the Chinese writing system, they saw words and meaning. When Kong-sang looked at them, they looked like lines that never seemed to sit still or come together. His teachers didn't seem to know what to do with him. They lectured him about his performance on tests and sighed in despair about his messy handwriting.

So it might have been because of his grades that he found himself standing in front of the Master Yu of the Chinese Opera Research Institute. Or it might have been because of his restlessness. Or maybe, probably, it was for some reason he knew nothing about. Kong-sang didn't ask why when his parents left him at the boarding school. He didn't ask why when they asked him to sign a ten year contract that would legally bind him to the school until he was 17. And he didn't ask why when they moved to Australia without him. Kong-sang just cried for a while and then tried to make them proud.

At first, the Chinese Opera Research Institute was an exciting place. From some rooms came the sounds of traditional Chinese musical instruments. From others came the sound of singing, from still others students discussing costuming. Around any corner could be two students rehearsing a mock sword fight or a group of students practicing back flips. The sole purpose of the school was to provide actors, musicians, and support personnel for traditional Chinese opera troupes. While some students learned to write music, others learned to direct. Kong-sang and his class learned singing, acting, acrobatics and martial arts.

To say that the Institute was hard did not begin to express the pain and exhaustion. The very first day, one of the teachers commanded him to do the splits. Kong-sang spread his legs side to side and sank as low as he could. He got his behind about eight inches off the ground and got stuck. His legs just wouldn't go any farther apart.

"Lower," he teacher commanded.

Kong-sang tried to sink lower, but his muscles tightened. The teacher came up behind him, and pressed down on his shoulders, forcing him deeper into the splits. Kong-sang gritted his teeth and held back the tears. One day the students would practice punches and kicks. The next they would sing. Some days they worked up elaborate routines with swords and spears. Other days they practiced applying the makeup that traditional Chinese opera actors wore. If they performed well, nobody said anything. If they failed, a teacher would take a cane to them or would make them stand on their hands in the corner until their arms quivered.

They must have gotten enough food because they continued to grow, but Kong-sang couldn't remember the last time he felt truly full. After a full day of training, he would strip down to his underwear, fall into his narrow cot with no mattress, put a threadbare blanket over him and despite his aching muscles, fall asleep instantly. One day followed the last, each full of challenges, punishments, and work harder than he'd ever known in his life.

When Kong-sang had been at the institute for a few years, the master came into the room and announced it was time for them to perform. The next evening, they got into costumes, painted their faces, and for the first time performed all the things they had been practicing in front of an audience. The audience applauded. But after the performance, on the way home, the master informed them that they had been so bad he was embarrassed to know them. When they got back to the institute everyone got five strokes of the cane. What they didn't get was their pay. All the money they had made on the performance went to the school. That was how his life was for ten years. When a nearby a community center wanted an opera performance, the students packed up their gear and went to perform. When a movie producer needed someone to play a beggar child in a movie, his school hired him out for the part. But mostly he practiced and learned, performed and heard how badly he had performed. He acted, and sang, and made money and never saw any of it.

He was seventeen when he finally graduated. At the Chinese Opera Research Institute, everyone got ten strokes with the cane at graduation. Kong-sang put on three pairs of pants and presented himself to the master. The master told him he was spared. Kong-sang gathered his few belongings and walked out the front door. He felt like he was being released from prison. For ten years, he had never left the school without the supervision of a teacher.

That's when he learned that there was almost no work in Traditional Chinese Opera. Before television and movies, Chinese opera was a big part of the entertainment in the country. Now it was considered something for old people and special occasions. After all that training, Kong-sang struggled to find work. For a while, he got a job as a kitchen helper. He did some construction work. When he could, he took bit parts in the kung fu movies that were becoming increasingly popular in Hong Kong, and he dreamed of someday becoming a star.

The movie producers called him a stunt monkey and gave him a stage name, so he wasn't even credited as Kong-sang. He was hired to take punches and do the stunts that the more important actors thought too dangerous. He had bruises all over his body, and every now and then he broke a bone. But he was learning the business, and after all, he was no stranger to pain. As he had done in school, he settled in to do the job in front of him and do it well despite the exhaustion and discomfort. More than anything he wanted to be great, a great actor, a great stuntman. He wanted to be the kind of person that would make his family proud.

It was 1973, and Kong-sang was 17. He had been hired to play a prison thug. The role was uncredited and short, but he got to be a stunt man for Bruce Lee, a superstar at the height of his career. Kong-sang's role was to charge Bruce Lee. Lee would pretend to hit him with a stick, and Kong-sang was supposed to fall. When the time came, Kong-sang ran in. Instead of pretending, Lee actually made contact and hit Kong-sang in the side of the head. Kong-sang went down. He was fine, but instead of getting up off-camera, he stayed down. When the director called cut, Bruce Lee ran over.

"Are you all right?" he asked.

Kong-sang was fine. He was young, strong, and he had been hit with sticks many times before at the institute. But instead of saying so, he held his head and moaned. He was enjoying Bruce Lee's attention.

"I'll be fine," he said, acting like someone who had nearly had his head broken. Lee nodded, a look of respect in his eye.

Later when they were done filming for the day, Bruce Lee came over to ask Kong-sang his name and to see how he was doing. They began to talk—about the movie, Kong-sang's martial arts style, finally his performance on the set.

"You're good," Lee said. "You could go far."

It turned out Bruce Lee was right. In 1976, Kong-sang was hired to star in his first leading role. The film was "Shaolin Wooden Men." When the producer asked him how he wanted to be credited, Kong-sang decided to use his real surname and "Jackie," a nickname he had been given while working in construction. It would soon be a name known around the world: Jackie Chan.

The story of Mu-lan comes from a poem written in northern China in the sixth century. It is probably not a true story. But it has been told over and over again for fourteen centuries because it reflects a courage and a devotion to family that inspires people no matter their time or place. Filmmakers in China, Taiwan, Hong Kong, and the United States have all made movies about this remarkable young woman.

The Ballad of Mu-lan

Mu-lan was fifteen years old. She lived in a China that expected her to marry, to raise a family, and to care for her parents in their old age. It most certainly did not expect her become a soldier and march off to war. In fact, waging war would have been the last thing Mu-lan herself expected to do with her life—until the day the soldiers arrived.

It was a quiet afternoon, and Mu-lan was weaving in the front room when the soldiers arrived with draft posters. Quietly, she left her work to look out the door and watch them trot into the yard atop their powerful horses. Her father stepped out into the courtyard to meet them. One of the soldiers handed him a rolled up scroll, a draft poster.

"Your family," the leader announced, "will be required to provide one man for the Khan's army. The fight against the invaders in the north has grown much worse. We must have soldiers to repel them, or our homes will be overrun."

"I understand," her father said. "Yet I have only three children, two girls who are seventeen and fifteen, and a son who is six years old. I would consider it an honor to serve the Khan myself, but I am no longer young, and my health is failing. I doubt I could serve well."

"That is not my concern," the soldier said. "And it shouldn't be yours either. Your duty is not to question the Khan's orders. Your duty is simply to obey. Within three days, you must send a member of your family to the army camp near the Yellow River. When he has left, tack this poster to your front gate. It will tell us that you have done your duty."

"Of course," Mu-lan's father said. "It will be an honor to serve."

The soldiers wheeled their horses around and headed down the road to the next house. Mu-lan's father turned slowly, clutching the poster in his hand. From her hiding place just inside the front door, Mu-lan could see his face. It was the color of ashes.

All that night Mu-lan tossed and turned, sleeping fitfully, seeing her father's ashen face in her dreams. When she awoke the next morning, she knew what she had to do. Her father was not well enough to join the army. He would not last even a month of riding hard, sleeping on the ground, eating the poor rations of a soldier. If she wanted to save her father's life, she would have to go to war herself.

So that morning, Mu-lan got up and put on her best clothes. Her mother, sister, and brother were outside feeding the animals. Her father was sitting on the front step staring into space. Quietly she lifted the floorboard under which Father kept his money. She pulled out the small sack and counted out a few coins. Gathering up some of her weaving, she told Mother she was going to go to the market to sell it.

Mu-lan went to the East Market and sold the weaving. A man there was selling a horse, a beautiful, spirited chestnut mare. She was the perfect horse, but Mu-lan knew if she went to purchase her, the man would wonder why a young girl was buying a horse. Mu-lan wandered the market until she found one of the draft-age boys who had come up from the camp. She hired him to purchase the horse for her. The boy was suspicious too, but he didn't turn down the pocket money she offered for his services.

Mu-lan led the horse to the West Market, where she bought a saddle, then to the South Market to buy a bridle, and the North Market to buy a whip. She didn't want anyone to suspect that she was outfitting herself for military duty. A few clerks raised eyebrows at Mu-lan's purchases. She told them she was buying equipment for her father. In a sense it was true. What she did, she did for him.

Satisfied that she had everything she needed, Mu-lan returned home. She tied the horse in the woods. She hid the saddle and bridle under the house. Then she snuck into her father's closet and took a change of clothes and hid it under her blankets. She would be ready to go in the morning.

That evening was unlike any Mu-lan had ever experienced in her life. For the first time, she looked and really saw her family. Her mother was cooking supper. Her sister was playing with her brother in the corner. Her father sat quietly, sharpening his sword, a look of deep sadness on his face. Mu-lan tried to etch their faces into her memory, to remember always what they looked like on that evening. More than anything, she wanted to gather them all into her arms and tell them how much she would miss them. But they couldn't know. Not yet.

The next morning Mu-lan rose early, long before even the first glimmer of light appeared on the horizon. She put on her father's clothes, shifting within them, trying to make them feel natural. No matter how she adjusted them, they still felt strange. She took her father's sword from its place and lashed the scabbard to her belt. Then she took the draft poster from the shelf. As she went out the front gate, she tacked it to the gatepost. The poster and the missing sword would be enough to tell her parents what she had done.

A lump rose in her throat as she gathered her saddle and bridle. With a great act of will, she turned her head and left behind the only home she had ever known.

The army camp by the Yellow River was already humming with activity when Mu-lan got there. The soldiers were a disorganized, ragged lot. Some of the older men had fought invaders the last time they had swarmed through the land. They were taking the younger soldiers aside and giving them advice about what to bring and what to leave behind. Some of the younger men wandered about, their faces sometimes beaming with bravado, sometimes clouded with dread. The youngest among them were little more than boys, thirteen, fourteen, or fifteen years old. Mu-lan was relieved to see that she was by no means the smallest one there.

That afternoon she met her commanders. That evening she slept on the ground, lulled to sleep by the sound of the river and the dull drone of hundreds of soldiers snoring in the cool air. She awoke several times during the night, each time straining her ears to hear the sound of her parents' voices. She was sure they would try to find her, to bring her back home. But when the dawn broke and the army saddled up to ride, Mu-lan scanned the crowd and saw only her fellow soldiers, their families clinging to them, begging them to do their duty and then come home.

For ten years Mu-lan rode with the army. For ten years and ten thousand miles. She saw terrors she knew she would never be able to tell her family, even if wanted to remember such fearful things, which she didn't. She saw friends die of disease, of wounds, of the cold and meager mountain air. Summer and winter, she slept on the hard ground, lulled to sleep by the whinnies of Mount Yen's wild horses. Some mornings, far too many mornings, she awoke to the blood-freezing war cries of a barbarian army. She outlived three generals. And while marching through mountain passes, laden with the armor of a man, she became a woman.

After ten years, the war was over. Those who survived were brought to the Splendid Hall. The Khan himself handed out promotions and awards. One of Mu-lan's friends was made a commander. Another was given a medal and made a secretary to a high official. When Mu-lan's turn came, she stepped before the Khan and bowed. The Khan hung a medal around her neck and handed her a scroll listing her acts of heroism and expressing the nation's gratitude.

"I wish to make you one of my ministers," he said. "Would that please you?"

"Thank you, sir," Mu-lan said. "But what would please me most is to return to my family. I have been gone far too long."

"I understand," the Khan said. "Go to them with my blessing."

Mu-lan met her friends outside the hall. "Come to my home this evening," she said. "We will feast and celebrate your new positions and my return to my family."

It was a short walk to Mu-lan's home. The way was familiar but like something out of a dream. As she approached her family's front gate, her knees began to shake. Her stomach tried to flap its way out of her body. Her breath floated in and out of her chest in fits and starts. Would her family recognize her after all those years? Certainly they would. Would they honor her for what she did, or would they turn their back on her and her deception, forcing her into the street to fend for herself? Mu-lan straightened the Khan's medal on her chest, clutched the emperor's scroll in her right hand, and pushed open the gate.

In the open door of the front room, Mu-lan's mother sat weaving. She looked up. Mu-lan's heart sank when she saw the lines that years of worry had left on her face. Her mother's hair was beginning to gray. She looked older, ten years older, maybe even twenty. As she looked up from her weaving, she saw Mu-lan's uniform and went pale. She cast a quick glance at a young man who had come around from the side of the house to see who had arrived. Mu-lan recognized his eyes. The young man was her brother. Of course. Mu-lan's mother would be worried that the soldier standing in the courtyard was here to draft him. Mu-lan tucked the scroll inside her sleeve.

"Mother," she said. It was all she could say before a lump rose in her throat.

"Mu-lan?"

Mu-lan nodded and went to her. She put her arms around her and felt her cheek against her own.

"Mu-lan," her mother said again.

Mu-lan's brother left and returned with their sister and father. Mu-lan handed the scroll to her father, then removed the medal from around her neck and hung it around his. Tears welled up in his eyes.

She went to her old room and took off her armor and her soldier's clothing. She washed the trail dust from her body and hair. Then she dabbed on some of her sister's perfume and powdered her face with flower powder. She took her old clothes from where they had been hanging in the corner, put them on, and fixed her hair. It had been a long time—ten long years of sleeping in armor and attending to her clothing only when battles and marches allowed. Mu-lan looked in the mirror. The woman who looked back pleased her.

Mu-lan's companions came that evening. She met them by torchlight at the gate. At first they looked right past her, scanning the courtyard for a young soldier in armor. But when Mu-lan spoke, their eyes widened.

This woman in silks and perfume was the soldier they had fought beside for ten years. They stood rooted to the path, staring despite themselves.

"Come in my friends," Mu-lan said. "Let's eat, and drink, and toast our new lives."

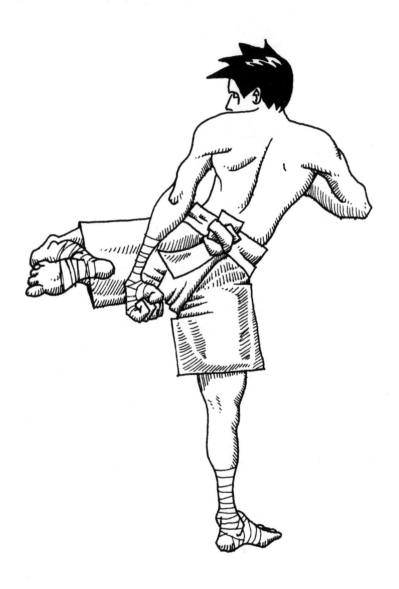

Muay Thai is sometimes called Thai boxing. Using hands, feet, knees, elbows, and shins, a Thai boxer batters an opponent until he is unable to continue. Because the sport is so demanding, Thai boxers spend a good deal of time and energy strengthening their body to be able to withstand punishment. They are some of the toughest fighters in the martial arts.

To this day, Muay Thai fighters dedicate one of their fights each year to a man named Nai Khanom Tom, a fighter who lived centuries ago, back when Thailand was still called Siam.

A Muay Thai Master Fights Twelve Burmese Warriors

"Who is that man?" the king of Burma demanded as he looked out over the battlefield. "The man in front of the Siamese charge. Who is he?"

The king's aide looked where the king was pointing. It was not difficult to see which man the king meant. In the front of the battle, where the fighting was heaviest, a single man was dropping Burmese soldiers one after another. "Your highness," the aide said, "that is Nai Khanom Tom."

"Nai . . . what was that again?" The king could not take his eyes off the magnificent fighter.

"Nai Khanom Tom."

"And why is it that none of my troops seem to be able to defeat him?" the king asked.

"Well, sir," his aide stumbled for words, not wanting to insult the king's troops. "Some say that Nai Khanom Tom is not even mortal. He is Siam's greatest boxer, and has never lost a fight. Some say he cannot die, that he was sent by the gods."

"Hmmph," the king said. "All men die. Even kings die. Send in the right warrior to oppose him, and you'll see that this Nai person can die, too."

"Yes, your highness," the aide replied meekly. The two watched as Nai Khanom Tom continued to cut through Burmese soldiers like rice stalks in the field.

"Mmm, that is something I'd like to see," the king said. "I'd like to see Nai face my great boxers. I'd like to see him beg for mercy."

A few weeks later, the king of Burma stood before two hundred of his most powerful soldiers. Some carried elephant spears, long spears with tips sharp enough to pierce elephant hide. Others carried ropes and nets.

"You are not to kill him," the king commanded. "If I hear that this Nai person died in battle, you will all pay dearly. Is that clear?"

The troops bowed their heads in obedience.

"I want him alive. Bring him to me." The king spun on his heel and strode back into the palace. The two hundred soldiers left to join the battle with Siam.

The soldiers brought Nai Khanom Tom in on a pole. His wrists were tied together. So were his ankles. A large pole was threaded between them. Four soldiers had loaded the pole onto their shoulders. They carried Nai Khanom Tom into the king's presence like a slain animal.

"He's not dead, is he?" the King demanded.

"No, sir," the captain replied. "He's a bit banged up. We had some trouble capturing him. Even after we tied his arms, he managed to take down two of my men with his knees."

"With his knees?" the king shouted. "Hmmph. Is that why you have him trussed up like a pig?"

"Yes, sir," the captain answered.

"Set him down," the king said, motioning to the troops carrying the pole. "Set him down right here."

"So, Nai . . . whatever your name is," the king said looking down at Nai Khanom Tom lying bound on the floor, "is it true what they say about you being a god?"

Nai Khanom Tom didn't answer. His eyes locked on the king's in a stare of complete calm and complete confidence. The king felt a shiver up his spine. He clasped his hands behind his back and made his way around to Nai Khanom Tom's other side.

"They say you don't fight like a mere man. You certainly have gone through enough of my troops."

Still Nai Khanom Tom was silent.

"How would you like the opportunity to earn your freedom?" The king continued to pace.

"How?" Nai Khanom Tom asked quietly.

"I think we have his interest," the king said brightly to his troops. The troops laughed appreciatively. "By fighting," the king said to Nai Khanom Tom.

"I will not fight in your army," Nai Khanom Tom said simply.

"Not in my army," the king said loudly. "He thought I wanted him to fight in my army." The troops again laughed obediently. "No, not in my army. At my festival. I want you to fight my best Bando fighters at my next festival. If you win, I'll set you free. 'In my army.' Mmmph. Are you sure you're some kind of god? You don't seem very bright to me."

Nai Khanom Tom lay silently on the floor. If the jeers of the king and his troops had any effect on him, it didn't show. The king made his way back to his dais.

"Do you agree?" he asked. "Will you fight?"

"Yes," said Nai Khanom Tom. "I'll fight your Bando fighters."

"Good. Very good," the king said. "Now, how many fighters should we have him fight? Four? Five?"

"I have nine that I have been training," the captain volunteered.

"Nine, you say," the king exclaimed. "Could you fight nine men, one after another, Siamese?"

Nai Khanom Tom was silent.

"What? Not enough?" The king motioned for his aide. "I want you to find the ten best Bando fighters in the kingdom. No, wait. Make that the fourteen best fighters. Ten might not be enough for this 'god' here."

The ring where Nai Khanom Tom would fight was roped off. The king entered the arena with his aide and the captain of his troops. He took his place in time to see Nai Khanom Tom making his way around the ring, touching each rope, whispering to himself.

"What is he doing?" the king said to his aide.

"He is sealing the ring," the aide said. "It keeps out evil spirits."

"Evil spirits will be the least of his worries," the king muttered.

Nai Khanom Tom returned to his corner of the ring. He knelt, touching his hands first to his forehead, then to the ring, then to his forehead, then to the ring, then to his forehead, then to the ring. A look of peace covered his face. He stood and began his ritual dance. The king watched as Nai Khanom Tom lifted first one knee, then the other. His movements were catlike, like a tiger, or maybe a leopard. He stretched and clawed, then turned to catch the eye of his opponent on the other side of the ring. The two locked eyes.

"Who is our first fighter?" the king asked the captain.

"The first fighter is one of my students, your majesty. He is young, but he is tough. He has an ability to wear down an opponent more thoroughly than any other man I've trained. He may not defeat Nai Khanom Tom, but I can guarantee you that after fighting my boy, Nai Khanom Tom will be lucky to still be standing halfway through his next fight."

"Good," said the king. "I'd enjoy seeing him so tired he could barely move. The man has far too much energy for my taste."

Nai Khanom Tom and the young fighter faced each other. Then like lightning, the knees began to fly. Nai Khanom Tom landed an elbow, then a knee. As he pulled out, the young fighter followed him with a flurry of knee strikes to Nai Khanom Tom's thighs and hips.

The fight wore on. It made the king tired just watching the punishment the two men were giving each other. He reached down to pick up his glass and ask for a refill. A gasp went up from the crowd. The king looked up. The young fighter was down.

"What was that?" he said.

"Nai Khanom Tom has injured my fighter's knee," the captain said.

"How did he do that?"

"He waited until the foot was planted, and then he kicked it with his shin," the captain replied.

"With his shin?" the king said, imagining the conditioning Nai would have had to do to use his shins as weapons.

The captain nodded.

"Well, if your man can't fight anymore, get him out of the ring," the king commanded. "I want someone else in there fighting right away."

"Yes, sir." The captain rose and, motioning for two of his men to follow, walked to the ring.

"How many has he fought?" the king asked, returning to his place.

"He's getting ready to face his ninth," said the captain. "It's been six hours." Admiration shone through in his voice.

"Who's your biggest, strongest man?" the king asked. "Send him in. This has gone on long enough." The captain bowed his head and stood to approach the fight master.

The fight master whispered in his assistant's ear, and his assistant ran off, returning with a man large enough to be two men. Nai Khanom Tom simply stood in the center of the ring and waited as the giant stepped over the ropes and removed his shirt.

"Perhaps the man never tires," the king murmured to his captain when he returned. "But I would be willing to bet that he breaks. It looks like your boy there is just the fellow to do the job."

The fighters squared off, Nai Khanom Tom dwarfed by the giant lumbering toward him. He snuck inside the big man's guard and elbowed furiously at his ribs, but the great bear of a man didn't seem to feel the strikes at all. Instead he grabbed Nai Khanom Tom and squeezed him so tightly that Nai Khanom Tom's face turned red.

"That's got him," the king said, clapping his hand in pleasure.

"Yes, your highness," his captain replied. But the captain saw weaknesses the king had obviously missed. Nai Khanom Tom saw those weaknesses, too. He stomped down hard on the giant's foot, then elbowed back into him. The giant bent over in pain. Like lightning, Nai Khanom Tom struck, a quick blow to the giant's head perhaps. The blow was far too quick to be seen clearly. The giant dropped to the mat, dazed.

"What did he do?" the king asked.

"I'm not sure, your highness," the captain said, "but it seems to have worked." The giant crouching on the floor of the ring was shaking his head, stunned and disoriented.

Cheers rose from the crowd. "Mmmph," the king said. "Since when do they cheer the enemy?"

"I believe, your highness," the captain said, "that they are simply cheering the superior fighter."

"Yes," said the king, "yes, I guess he is that."

Nai Khanom Tom was fighting his twelfth opponent. While his opponents lay exhausted and demoralized on the edges of the arena, Nai Khanom Tom was still on his feet, still dominating the ring. The king found himself respecting the brave man who continued to fight through exhaustion and pain. One would think that he wouldn't have the strength by now to lift even a finger. But yet he continued to throw punishing knees and elbows. He connected with a fierce elbow to his opponent's midsection. The man crumpled to the floor, the wind knocked out of him.

Nai Khanom Tom staggered to his corner and leaned against the post. His next opponent prepared to enter the ring.

"Enough," said the king, standing, then clapping his hands twice. "Twelve is enough. Nai Khanom Tom," he called loudly. "Come and stand before me."

Nai Khanom Tom left the ring. He wiped his face on a towel, then handed it to one of several men who had taken up a place in his corner of the ring. He breathed deeply, steadying his breath, then turned, squared his shoulders, and walked to where the king stood waiting for him.

The king looked into the fighter's eyes, wondering if he would recognize a god if he saw one. What the king saw was a resolve that made him take a step back. This fighter, even after twelve long, bloody fights, could still break him like a twig in mere seconds.

"Nai Khanom Tom," he said, pushing the fear he felt down deep where it could not affect his voice, "you have fought well. I am a man of my word. You will be given clean clothes and a chance to rest. Then my captain will personally escort you to the Siam border." Nai Khanom Tom bowed his head slightly. The king saw the muscles of his neck quiver as he did so.

"I have never seen a man fight like you did today," the king said more quietly. "Be assured that in Burma as well as in Siam, the name of Nai Khanom Tom will be remembered and spoken with respect for many generations."

Most traditional martial arts have their roots in Asia. Capoeira is one of the exceptions. This Afro-Brazilian art, which combines elements of combat, dance, acrobatics, and music, was invented in the 16th century by African slaves in Brazil. Its kicks and spins are some of the most athletic techniques in all the martial arts.

Zumbi: Capoeirista, Slave and King

Zumbi hated the name Francisco. He hated it partly because everyone called him that despite the fact it wasn't his name. But he really hated it because it was given to him by the man who had taken his freedom and made him a slave.

Zumbi's mother was central African nobility. His father was an Imbangala warrior from Angola. Both had been captured in Africa by Portuguese soldiers and brought to Brazil to work as slaves on a sugar plantation. Because of his father's fighting skills, Zumbi's parents were able to escape the brutal life of a plantation slave. They fled to a runaway-slave colony called Palmares. It was there that Zumbi was born, a free Afro-Brazilian.

But in the 17th century, freedom in Brazil could be a shaky thing. Free Brazilians of African descent could be snatched up at any time and sold into slavery. The indigenous people, Indians who had been in Brazil long before the Europeans arrived, could also be rounded up and sold to plantations to pick cotton. From as early as he could remember, Zumbi's parents had warned him about the dangers.

He was six years old, playing on the edge of the Palmares village when the soldiers came. Before the village warriors could be alerted, before his parents even knew he was missing, Zumbi was snatched up and whisked away to the city. There he was given to a Catholic priest by the name of Father António Melo. The first thing Father António did was take away Zumbi's clothes. He gave Zumbi the rough, shapeless linen shirt and trousers that marked a slave. Then he took Zumbi into the church, baptized him at the font, and told him that from then on, his name was Francisco.

The first night, Zumbi cried himself to sleep. The next day, he swore to himself that, like his father and mother before him, he would find a way to escape.

At Father António's house, Zumbi was a house boy. He cleaned the house and church, grew vegetables for the table. He helped the cook keep the cooking fires burning. He lifted and carried, cleaned and polished. He did smelly work like emptying Father António's chamber pot, and he did boring work like keeping birds from eating the food in the garden. Like plantation slaves, he worked sunup to sundown. But unlike children on plantations, Zumbi lived to see the next year and the year after that. Unlike the slave children of the plantations who died of disease and malnutrition, Zumbi lived, and his hard work made him strong.

Each day was pretty much the same. In the morning he went to church with Father António. He knelt as the Father said Mass. In the morning when the air was cooler, Zumbi did his heavy work. At around 11 o'clock he served at table for Father António and whatever guests had been invited that day. Father António always went to his study after mid-day meal. There he would pray his midday prayers, nap for a while, and then study his books. When he came out around 5 p.m. to say prayers at the church before supper, he would check to make sure Zumbi had done his afternoon work. If he had, Father António would say nothing. If he hadn't, Father António might take a switch to his legs or tell Cook not to feed him that night. The best thing about afternoons was that Zumbi could usually count on doing his work without Father António watching over his shoulder.

One day Father António called Zumbi into his study. "Francisco," he said, "do you know where the government offices are on the other side of town?"

"Yes, Father," Zumbi said.

"I want you to bring these dispatches to the office. Give them to the official at the front desk, and tell him they are from me. Tell him they need do go out on the next ship to Portugal."

"Yes, Father," Zumbi said. This was something new. He had been all over town with Father António, who figured he didn't need a burro when he had Zumbi to carry things. But he had never walked the city on his own. He remembered his promise to himself to escape as soon as he could.

"Come right back and clean the church when you are done," Father António said. "Don't go wandering."

"Yes, Father," Zumbi said.

Alone in the city, Zumbi couldn't help but feel that the world suddenly held so many more possibilities. He could take the main road across town, or he could take back streets. He could stop for a moment and look through open gates to see what other people were doing. Maybe he could even escape. He was beginning to make escape plans—considering whether he would need to bring food, speculating about which way Palmares might be, thinking about whether it would be best to travel by day or wait until after dark—when he looked through a gate and saw five African men in slave dress playing instruments and dancing. It was a strange dance, lots of crouching and swinging of legs this way and that. He watched for a few minutes and just as he was about to leave, he heard one of the men say something. It took him a moment before he realized that he understood what the man was saying even though the man wasn't speaking either Portuguese or Latin, the languages spoken at Father Antonio's house. His man was speaking his parents' language.

Without a second though Zumbi dashed into the courtyard and greeted the men in his own language. It had been a couple of years since he had spoken it, and feeling it on his tongue again felt sweet. The men asked him about his family. He told them everything he could remember.

"And what is the grandson of a princess doing in slave clothing?" the eldest man said.

"Trying to escape," Zumbi said, lifting his chin and thrusting his chest out.

The man laughed. "Aren't we all?" he said. "Come and train with us. We will teach you what you need to know to find your way back to Palmares. We 'dance' here in this courtyard every afternoon." The man's companions chuckled like they knew a secret Zumbi didn't know. "We are here during the heat of the day when our households are all napping. Come tomorrow, and we will teach you everything you need to win your freedom and keep it."

The next day Zumbi woke early. He did some of his morning work before Father António awoke. Then after Mass he hurried to do the rest of his morning work and some of his afternoon work as well. When the Father had retreated to his study and the cook had stretched out on the back porch for her afternoon nap, Zumbi snuck out the front gate and dashed across town to the courtyard he had visited the day before.

"Before we begin," the man everyone called Mestre said, "I must have your word."

Without hesitating, Zumbi nodded.

"I must have your word that you will never tell anyone what we do here," Mestre said.

"You have my word," Zumbi replied.

"The dance we do, the dance that the Portuguese see us do, is actually a very effective fighting system. We call it *Jogo de Capoeira*, the Capoeira Game. It's where we learn the basic techniques of our martial art."

Mestre nodded to the other men. They took up instruments and began to play and sing. "Do what I do," he said. He dropped his left foot back and brought his left arm up in front of his face. Zumbi copied him. Then Mestre brought his left foot forward and dropped his right foot back and brought his right arm up. Again, Zumbi copied him. They continued like this—right foot back, left foot back, right foot back, left foot back. The musicians continued to sing, and Zumbi felt the rhythm as his body moved in time with the beat of the drum.

"We call this the *ginga*," Mestre said. "It is the most fundamental movement in capoeira. Every time you come here, you will practice the ginga."

They practiced for a while, Zumbi and Mestre, facing each other, doing the ginga. Mestre nodded. One of the players set down his instrument.

"Just watch for now," Mestre said, motioning for him to join the musicians. "This is called the *roda*."

The player cartwheeled into place opposite Mestre. Zumbi recognized the *ginga*, but then the two players began to dodge and weave. Mestre jackknifed at the waist and swung his leg up and over, missing his student's head by inches. The student moved with the technique, swinging his own kick at Mestre.

Zumbi saw handstands, two handed and one handed. He saw sweeps and takedowns, rolls, ducks and cartwheels. Zumbi's eyes grew wide. What had been just a dance yesterday was suddenly a fight. He imagined if one of those wide sweeping kicks ever met its target. It could knock a person down with one blow. The kicks never landed, however. The players slipped them, ducked under them, moved with them.

When they finished, they packed up their instruments, and toweled themselves off. Zumbi went over to Mestre.

"Mestre," he said, "more than anything else I want to be able to dance and fight like you do."

"More than being free?" Mestre asked.

Zumbi froze for a moment, not knowing how to answer. What he had said was almost true. It was what he wanted more than anything else except freedom.

"Don't worry," Mestre said. "I won't make you choose." Zumbi sighed in relief. "I will, however, ask you to wait. I want you to train with me until you can succeed in your escape. Right now are you strong enough to make the walk through the wild areas between here and your parents? If you ran today, could you make your way through the soldiers and slave catchers that surround both the city and Palmares? Stay, and I will train you in capoeira, and I will teach you how to escape."

Zumbi was 15 years old when Mestre proclaimed him ready. Each day he trained, making the fighting techniques of capoeira his own. Every now and again, a new slave found his way into the courtyard. As Zumbi became more proficient, he helped train the newcomers. In exchange, Mestre taught him bushcraft and techniques for hiding and running silently through the rain forest. Then one day, after the *roda*, Mestre said, "It's time. Go. At your next opportunity, go. And give my regards to Palmares."

It wasn't hard for Zumbi to slip away. All the years he had been training, Zumbi had been a model servant. Father António trusted him, never realizing that Zumbi was doing his work so well for one reason only, to pave the way for his escape. Afternoon came. Father António retreated to his study. Zumbi snuck out of the compound as he always did. But this time, he just kept walking.

Using the tricks Mestre had taught him, he slipped past the soldiers outside the city. He crept through the rainforest like a big cat. He slept in trees, ate what the rainforest gave him, moved steadily, day after day toward Palmares.

On the outskirts of Palmares, not far from where he had been captured nine years earlier, Zumbi saw two soldiers, scanning the edge of the village for stragglers to capture. Zumbi's anger rose in him like a wild beast. Perhaps it was courage, perhaps only foolishness, but whatever it was, Zumbi stepped out from the cover of the trees, and stalked toward the soldiers. Zumbi was tall, as tall as any full-grown man, and he was strong from his years of training and work. The soldiers pulled their swords.

"Stop," one of them said. Zumbi continued to stride toward them. The closest one swung his sword. Zumbi moved with it, ducking and spinning. His heel came up, swung a wide arc and caught the soldier in the temple. The soldier dropped to the ground like a felled tree. Zumbi then set that foot down and brought the other one up, and the second soldier fell as well.

Zumbi strode into the village, a free man.

The leadership of the village of Palmares recognized Zumbi's skills as a martial artist. Soon he was training fighters. In his early 20s, he became commander in chief of the defense force. He lead raids to sabotage plantations and free the slaves. Many slaves owed their freedom to Zumbi and to the Village of Palmares, which took them in as fellow citizens.

When Zumbi was 32 years old, when he had been freeing slaves for more than a decade, the Portuguese governor contacted the king of Palmares. The governor offered all the runaways in the village amnesty and freedom if they would submit to Portuguese authority and stop trying to free more slaves. The king decided he would take the governor's offer. Zumbi was furious. He challenged the king to a fight, won the fight, and became king himself. Until his death in 1695 at age 50, Zumbi never rested in his efforts to free Brazilian slaves.

Today in Brazil, on every November 20th, Zumbi, the boy who was once a slave called Francisco, the man who refused to compromise with slave owners, is remembered as a wise king and celebrated as a freedom fighter and a hero.

Wing Chun is a Chinese martial art. It was developed over three hundred years ago by Ng Mui, a Buddhist nun in a Shaolin monastery. Ng Mui was a very small woman who found that she was not able to make standard martial arts techniques work against people much larger than she was. She didn't have a lot of muscle, weight, or a long reach. What she did have was speed and the ability to use an opponent's size against him. After learning her teacher's style thoroughly, she began modifying it to suit her needs. The result is what we now call Wing Chun, a quick efficient style named after one of Ng Mui's best students. This is the story of that student.

Wing Chun

Yim Wing Chun was in love. Her boyfriend, Leong Bok Chao, was handsome, intelligent, thoughtful, and, most of all, hopelessly in love with Wing Chun. He was also leaving on a long journey. That journey would take him away from the northern mountains, where Wing Chun lived, to Fukien in the southern part of China. It would take him across difficult terrain, through a region at war against the Manchurian occupation. He and Wing Chun would be apart for more than a year.

"When I return," Bok Chao said, "we will get married. I will set up a salt shop near your father's bean curd shop. We will work together and have beautiful children."

"Come home safely," Wing Chun said, holding his hand tightly to her heart. "I can't imagine a future without you."

Life for Wing Chun was lonely without Bok Chao. Since her mother died several months earlier, Wing Chun had done the cooking and cleaning for her father. During the afternoons she worked in the family shop. Having work to do was a comfort. Her mother had always told her that if she kept busy, the loneliness wouldn't hurt so badly. So she scrubbed the house and her father's shop until it shone. But life without either Bok Chao or her mother had a big hole right in the middle of it.

One day, Wing Chun was in the back of her father's shop making dao fu, a soft bean curd cheese. She heard her father in the front greet a customer warmly. The two struck up a conversation—her father did love to talk. The customer, a servant of a local warlord, noticed Wing Chun in the back of the shop.

"Is that your daughter?" the customer said.

Her father nodded. "Her name is Yim Wing Chun. It means 'beautiful springtime.'" His eyes were filled with pride.

"She is very beautiful," the customer commented, watching Wing Chun's every move.

"Yes," her father said. "And she has a wonderful gentle and giving spirit. I don't know what I would have done without her since her mother died."

"My lord is looking for a wife," the servant said. "He is very wealthy and very powerful. Your daughter would want for nothing."

"I am flattered," her father said, "but Wing Chun is engaged. She will marry Leong Bok Chao when he returns from Fukien. I'm sorry, but it has already been arranged."

"I see," said the servant. "A pity. I know my lord would find her very desirable."

The next day, Wing Chun was sweeping the shop when a large, elegantly armored man stepped up to the front window.

"Yim Wing Chun," he said gruffly, almost as though he were issuing a command.

"I am Yim Wing Chun," she said, setting aside her broom.

"Yes," the large man said to his servant, the man who had been at the shop the day before, "you were right. She will make a beautiful wife for me."

"Call your father," he said to Wing Chun. "The two of you will come with me. The wedding will be this afternoon."

"Sir, I'm engaged." Wing Chun said. "I can't marry you. I don't even know you."

"Yes, yes," he said impatiently. "That doesn't matter to me. I am a straightforward man. If I like something, I take it. If someone stands in my way, I go right over the top of him. I find it makes life much simpler.

Now call your father."

Wing Chun turned and began to walk home to get her father. She was eager to get away from the terrible man at the shop, and soon found her walk had turned into a stumbling trot and then a run. What an ugly, terrible, altogether nasty man, she thought. I can't marry him. I can't. I can't marry him. Lost in her thoughts and fear, she rounded the corner of a vegetable shop and almost ran into a woman buying a cabbage.

"I beg your pardon," Wing Chun said as she looked up to see the woman was a Buddhist nun.

"And what has you dashing through the market?" the nun asked, a gentle smile creasing her old face.

"I have to, I have to get my father," Wing Chun stammered. "He . . . I mean a man, a warlord . . . my father has to . . ."

"Slow down," the nun replied. "The warlord and your father are not here right now. Right now it is just you and I. There is nothing here that can hurt you. My name is Ng Mui. I am a nun at the White Crane Temple. Take a couple of deep breaths. If you will tell me what has you so upset, maybe I can help."

Wing Chun breathed in and out. Looking into the gentle face of the woman standing before her, she saw a deep calm. The tension drained from her body, and she began to cry. Before she knew it, she had told the kind nun the whole story about Bok Chao, her mother's death, the warlord.

"I see," said Ng Mui. "Let's go get your father. I think I may have a solution to your problem."

"So you see," Wing Chun's father said to the warlord sitting in their home. "I couldn't possibly arrange for a suitable wedding in less than a year's time."

Ng Mui looked on from the corner where she sat holding Wing Chun's hand. He was handling the situation just as she had coached him.

"I need some time to plan the feast. A great man like yourself should be honored properly on his wedding day. And I need to send word to Bok Chao breaking the engagement. With all the turmoil in the country, it could easily take a year to find him. Yes, I think a year would be appropriate. A year from today you will marry my daughter at a wedding that people will talk about for years to come."

"A year," said the warlord. "She had better be worth the wait."

"Oh, she will be," her father said.

"A year, then." The warlord stood, cast a quick glance at Wing Chun, spun on his heel, and left.

"That gives us a year to prepare," Ng Mui said. "Mr. Yee, please send a message to Bok Chao. Wing Chun, meet me tomorrow at dawn outside the gates of the temple. A year is none too long. We must work hard."

At dawn, Wing Chun walked the path up the hill to the monastery. Just outside the gates in a small garden she found Ng Mui. The old nun stood motionless, her feet about shoulder's width apart, knees bent, her right hand in a fist pulled back to her side at the waist, her left hand open in front of her chest. On her face was a look of complete concentration. As she watched, Wing Chun saw that the nun was not in fact standing motionless. Slowly, too slowly to be seen, her left hand inched steadily forward. Wing Chun sat down on a bench and watched fascinated.

Ng Mui finished her exercise. Her face damp with perspiration, she turned to Wing Chun and motioned for her to come.

"It's your turn to practice," she said. "I see now why I was sent here. I thought it was just bad luck when the war against the Manchurians drove me from my home. But I see now that I was sent here to teach you. You have a year to learn how to turn power, rudeness, and brute force against itself. Here. Stand like this."

Spring turned into summer. Each morning Wing Chun climbed the hill to the garden outside the monastery. Summer turned into fall. Her punches and kicks gained speed and power. Winter covered the garden with snow and ice, and Wing Chun learned to keep her feet under her center while moving quickly and effortlessly. Winter yielded to spring. The day of the wedding approached.

"It's time," Ng Mui said to Wing Chun on the day of their final lesson. "Send word to the warlord that we need to see him about some last minute details."

The warlord came into town sitting tall atop a powerful horse. Wing Chun looked up at him, at the heavy armor covering huge muscles, at the thickness of his neck and the size of his hands. He stepped down off his horse and walked over to where Wing Chun, her father, and Ng Mui stood.

"What is this 'last minute detail' that's so important that it couldn't wait until the wedding tomorrow?" If anything he had grown even uglier in the last year.

"It is a matter of honor," Ng Mui said stepping forward to meet him. "You see, Wing Chun is a member of a secret society of martial artists. As a part of her oath, she promised never to marry a man who could not defeat her in an unarmed fight."

"What!" the warlord shouted. "That's ridiculous. I have never heard of such a thing in my life."

"That's not surprising," Ng Mui said calmly. "Not many people have. The society is secret, after all."

"You're saying I have to fight her, fight this . . . puny little thing?"

"Yes," said Ng Mui. "She is, as you say, quite small. It should be no problem for a powerful man like you. A mere formality, really."

"Do you want this?" the warlord said to Wing Chun.

"I must, sir," she said. "I would be humiliated to marry someone who was not my equal."

"'Not your equal?' Not your equal? Such foolishness. I will be happy to flatten you, to teach you some respect for your future husband."

He waved over his servant, stripped off his sword and his armor, and piled them in his servant's arms. He rolled his head on his shoulders to loosen up.

"Let's finish this nonsense quickly. It would be a shame to mess up such a pretty face just before the wedding."

Wing Chun stepped out to the center of the street. She faced the warlord calmly. She nodded ever so slightly to him, then brought her hands up in front of her. A crowd began to gather.

The warlord closed the distance with a swagger. He put his hands up and charged, his hands grabbing for her waist. Wing Chun shifted her weight, slipped his attack, and at the last second swept his back foot out from under him. The warlord went sprawling into the dust. He stood, brushed the dirt from his knees, and glared at Wing Chun. She met his gaze with a look of calm concentration.

The warlord, more cautious this time, closed the distance again. Brushing down her guard with his front hand, he swung wildly at her head. Wing Chun used the downward momentum, ducked the punch, and came up under the warlord's ribs with a fast, hard punch. The warlord grunted in pain and staggered backward. Still clutching his ribs, he reached into his belt and drew out a dagger.

"I will kill you," he said, "before I will be beaten by you."

With a great cry he charged, driving the dagger toward Wing Chun's belly. Like a door opening, she pivoted on her heels, slipped the attack, and extended a punch at neck level. The force of the warlord's attack carried him into it, and it crashed into his throat with a force that picked him up off his feet.

Lying on the ground he gagged and gasped. His servants rushed to his aid. Ng Mui brushed them aside and knelt next to him. She pried his hands from his throat and examined him.

"He will live," she said. "Take him away. He is not worthy of my pupil."

The servants gathered up their master and carried him off.

A few days later Wing Chun was working at her father's shop. She looked up from the bean curd she was stirring to see Bok Chao looking down at her. A look of pain covered his face.

"Am I too late?" he asked. "Your father's note said the wedding was two days ago. Tell me I'm not too late."

"No, Bok Chao," she said. "Even if you had not come for another year, you would not be too late. I would wait a lifetime just for a few seconds as your wife."

He gathered her in his arms. "But the warlord . . ." he said.

"Will not bother us. I convinced him I was more trouble than I was worth."

"Then come with me, my wife to be. We have a lot to talk about."

Wing Chun and Bok Chao got married. They decided not to open the salt shop they had planned on, but rather joined the struggle against the Manchurian occupation. Wing Chun taught her husband all she knew about the martial arts. Together they taught students who soon came to call the style Wing Chun.

*T*amo has many names. The one name we don't know is the name his parents gave him when he was born in India more than fifteen hundred years ago. In China, though, he is called Tamo, in India Bodhidharma, in Japan Taishi Daruma. He introduced Zen to China, and he developed the exercises that later became chuan fa, the ancestor of many of today's Asian martial arts styles.

The Eighteen Hands, Ancestor of the Chinese Martial Arts

Tamo, the one they call the White Buddha, once walked all the way from India to China to visit the Chinese emperor and the Buddhist temples there. With him he brought a new way of living called Zen. Eventually, Zen would reach every corner of China and then find its way to Japan. But when Tamo first arrived in China, Zen simply made him an outcast.

It seems that when Tamo arrived at the royal palace, the emperor bragged to him about the monasteries he had built, about the scrolls his monks had translated from Sanskrit to Chinese, and about the way he was bringing Buddhism to the people. Tamo, never one to mince words, told the emperor that all these good efforts would not earn him Nirvana. He tried to tell the emperor about Zen. But the emperor branded Tamo a troublemaker and kicked him out of his palace.

Tamo traveled for a while, then arrived at the gate of a monastery. The abbot of the monastery had already been warned by imperial messengers that Tamo might show up. So when Tamo knocked at the gate, the abbot turned him away. Tamo was not upset. He simply climbed the hill outside the monastery and sat down in a cave to meditate.

In the morning, when the light was right, the monks could see him there from the window of their scriptorium, the place where they translated and copied Sanskrit scrolls. Never moving, he sat, his eyes focused on a single place on the cave wall.

Eventually, the abbot sent a young monk to the cave with food.

When he returned, the monk said that he could feel the force from Tamo's eyes as it bounced off the cave walls. In fact, the monk reported, if you looked carefully, you could see where Tamo's gaze had worn small holes in the cave wall. The young monk's words spread like a fire through the monastery. The next day, the abbot sent an older monk with the food instead. When he returned, the monks asked him if what the young monk said was true. He only replied that he would not engage in idle gossip.

Tamo remained in the cave for a long time. Every day the monks saw him in the same place, the same position, staring at the wall. Respect for him grew. So did the rumors. Finally, the abbot decided that Tamo should come down and talk to the monks. Maybe the abbot respected Tamo's abilities. Maybe he just wanted his gossiping monks to see that this man was merely human, like they were. Whatever his reasons, the abbot brought Tamo into the compound, and from that day nothing was ever the same.

Tamo showed the monks how to meditate, how to sit quietly on the floor, hands in their laps, eyes fixed on a single point. He taught them how to watch their breath going in and out, how to clear their minds, and take in the energy from the world around them. The monks tried. They tried very hard. A few could meditate from the time the sun first appeared over the horizon to the time it was straight overhead. Most drifted off to sleep after a hundred or two hundred breaths. For all of them, sitting for hours was painful and very frustrating.

One day the abbot and Tamo were walking together through the monastery grounds, talking about the trouble the monks were having with their meditation. They walked through the scriptorium, where dozens of monks sat bent over desks translating and copying. A few napped at their desks. One monk put a hand to his neck and grimaced, rubbing it and moving it back and forth. His neck seemed to have a permanent bend in it.

"Are all your monks in such poor shape?" Tamo asked the abbot.

"Well," said the abbot, "mostly they just sit and translate. It is hard on the body, but it is a worthwhile way to spend one's life."

"Yes, no doubt, no doubt," Tamo replied. "But if I could find a way for your monks to meditate better and do their work better, would you be interested?"

"Certainly," said the abbot, "What do you have in mind?"

"I'll let you know when I have all the details worked out," Tamo replied.

The next day out the scriptorium window, the monks saw Tamo on the hill again. This time, however, he was moving around outside the mouth of his cave. The movements were strange, like dance, but not like dance.

"He looks like a snake," said one of the monks.

"Perhaps he has been possessed by the spirit of a snake," said another.

"That's silly," said a third, a tall monk who was able to see over the top of the others. "I can see it better than you can. It's just a dance, a snake dance maybe."

"It doesn't look like a dance to me," said the first. "It doesn't have the rhythm of a dance."

"Sure it does," said the tall monk. "It's you who have no rhythm."

The only thing the monks could agree on was that Tamo's movement seemed full of life. Something about it—the grace, the energy, maybe the power—drew them in and made them want to be able to do the same thing themselves.

A few months later, the abbot called the monks together. Tamo had something he wanted to present.

"It's called 'The Eighteen Hands of the Lohan,'" he said. "Another name is 'Those Who Subdue or Attain Victory over Foes.' I learned something like it in my youth. My father wanted me to be a soldier, and so I trained in the weaponless combat arts in India."

"Wait," said the abbot. "You didn't say anything about training my monks to be soldiers."

"I have no intention of making them into soldiers," Tamo replied. "It would be a shame to waste such fine translators and scholars on war, just as it would be a waste of good soldiers to put them behind a desk." He smiled at the monks, who smiled warily back at him. "The enemy in this case is weakness and sickness. A weak and sick translator cannot do his job. A weak and sick monk cannot stay awake to meditate. To fight weakness, we must grow the chi within you. Let me show you."

Tamo stepped out to an open space in the midst of the group. His face grew quiet. Slowly he began to move. His legs became snakes. Then his fingers made a bird's beak. His hands struck the air fast and hard like the paws of a leopard, then whipped through the air like the wings of a dragon. Right there, in the courtyard of the monastery, Tamo was transformed into animal energy.

"Do you ever see the animals fall asleep during their work?" Tamo asked. "Have you ever seen a snake coil to strike its prey and then suddenly drift off into a nap?" The monks chuckled. "It is because the animals know how to gather, store, and use chi, the energy of the universe. Once you learn the same thing, you too will move with the power of the tiger. You will be able to remain alert while standing motionless like the crane. Come," he said, "Let me show you."

That was hundreds of years ago. Several years after Tamo left the monastery, he traveled all the way to Japan teaching Zen and the Eighteen Hands. His students taught other students, and they in turn taught other students. Soon people all over East Asia were doing the Eighteen Hands. Today, more than fifteen hundred years later, people all over the world still practice martial arts that can be traced back to Tamo.

Martial artists have learned much from watching animals fight. From the snake we can learn fluidity, from the tiger power, and from the crane the ability to fight on one leg. In this story, a samurai learns a valuable lesson from the unlikeliest of animals: a sleeping cat.

The Samurai and the Zen-Master Cat

Once there was a samurai who had a rat problem. The rat was a wily little beast who lived under the samurai's house. Several times a day, the rat would creep up into the house where it ate the samurai's food, chewed the samurai's good clothing, and frightened the samurai's family.

The samurai's servants tried chasing it away with a broom. The samurai's children tried shouting and throwing rocks at it. Finally, the samurai tried hunting it with a spear. None of them had any success. No matter what they did, the rat stayed just out of range until the family turned its back. Then it would go back to chewing the samurai's clothing and eating his food.

Finally, the samurai decided it was time to call in a specialist. He went to his neighbor's house and asked to borrow the neighbor's cat.

"My cat will catch that rat," the neighbor said. "She's young, and strong, and extremely fast. I've seen her catch prey almost twice her size. She'll have that rat under her claws before sunset."

So the samurai carried the cat home. They found the rat in the kitchen sitting right in the middle of the floor, nibbling a little bit of leftover tofu. The cat bolted from the samurai's arms. She was on the rat in a flash. Somehow, though, the rat broke free and dashed behind a water bucket. The cat followed. Behind the bucket, over a sack of rice, twice around the cook who jumped from foot to foot trying to avoid getting tangled up in the streak of fur and claws. Finally, the rat bolted for the door, and the cat pursued it into the yard.

The samurai was pleased. That cat was indeed fast. Her paws were like lightning, so fast that the samurai was a bit jealous of her speed. No doubt the rat was not long for this world.

That evening, the samurai sat down to supper with his family. He was enjoying an especially nice piece of grilled fish when he looked up, and there in the doorway, watching the family eat, was the rat.

The next day the samurai went to his neighbor's house. The cat lay by the fire nursing a nasty rat bite in her front leg.

"She came back last night," the neighbor said. "She was dirty, exhausted, and licking that bite in her leg."

"The rat is still at my house," the samurai said.

"I'm so sorry for my cat's poor performance," the neighbor said, bowing deeply. "If I might suggest, maybe you should try the fishmonger's cat. He's a big brute of a cat. He's been keeping the mice from the fishmonger's shop for several years now. Maybe he can handle your rat."

So the samurai talked to the fishmonger, who handed him a twenty-pound tomcat. The cat was all muscle and smelled a bit like fish. The samurai carried the tom home and released him at the front door. The old tom strolled through the house casually, then found a sack in the kitchen and hid behind it. A couple of hours later, the rat strolled by. The cat pounced. The rat escaped. The cat went back to waiting. All evening long, the cat hid and pounced, hid and pounced. As the old cat learned the rat's maneuvers, the cat's ambushes became more elaborate. He trapped the rat against the wall, herded it into corners, pinched it between two water buckets. The samurai admired the cat's skill, for though the cat expended very little effort, he was executing ambushes worthy of any general.

Yet after every ambush, the rat escaped.

One day passed, then two. The old tom continued to stalk its prey. But the rat was slippery and the cat could not lay so much as a claw on it. Finally, at the end of the week, the samurai packed up the cat and brought him back to the fishmonger.

That evening at the Zen temple after meditation, the samurai vented his frustration to one of the monks.

"You should try our cat," the monk said. "She is a rat master." The monk pointed to an old, scruffy-looking cat curled up by the fire. The samurai was doubtful. But since he had no better idea, he brought her home. The cat immediately found the fire and fell asleep beside it. The next day after breakfast, she found a sunbeam on the porch and napped there until supper, after which she returned to her place by the fire.

After a week of napping and eating, eating and napping, the cat still hadn't even looked at the rat much less chased it. The samurai scooped her up, barely waking her from her nap, and carried her back to the temple.

"Have patience," the monk said. "She's a master ratter. She knows what she's doing." So the samurai returned her to his house and her place by the fire and waited. A week passed, then two weeks. The rat, meanwhile was getting bolder. It jumped up on the table to eat the food. It got into the closet and slept on the futons. It paid no more attention to the cat than it would a rug by the fire.

One day, the rat was making its way to a plate of food waiting to be cooked over the fire. Not thinking twice, it scurried right in front of the sleeping cat. Instantly, the cat pounced. It grabbed the rat by the scruff of the neck and shook it. The rat fell dead at the cat's feet.

The samurai returned the cat to the temple the next day. "You are right," he said. "She succeeded in a way neither of the other cats could. She is indeed a master ratter."

"And what did the master teach you?" the monk asked.

The samurai thought for a moment. "There is a time to strike and a time to wait," the samurai finally said. "A wise warrior knows the difference."

Miyamoto Musashi at his death was considered the greatest sword fighter in the history of Japan. He never lost a fight in a contest with another sword fighter. He also authored the Book of Five Rings, *a strategy manual still widely read today.*

The Mind Is a Sword

The young Miyamoto Musashi was a good swordsman, no doubt about that. But on the day he met Seijuro, Musashi was still young and largely untested. Seijuro, on the other hand, was one of the greatest sword masters in the entire country. His reputation as both a teacher and a ruthless fighter had grown in the more than twenty years he had been fighting.

Musashi, who was only nineteen years old, had issued a challenge and was going to fight him at sunrise.

As Musashi roamed the town the day before the fight, he went over in his mind everything he knew of Seijuro, his personality, and his strategy. He knew that Seijuro had a fiery temperament and the fast, hard techniques to match it. He easily maimed or killed opponents in the past. Yet Musashi believed he could win. If he could keep his wits about him, he could win.

Musashi stopped at a noodle shop. Bowing politely to the shopkeeper, he asked for a bowl of soba. Leaning against a narrow counter, he ate the noodles. When he finished, he handed to bowl back to the shopkeeper.

"Come see me fight," he said. "I will be fighting Seijuro Sensei tomorrow morning in the field on the north end of town. Come watch. And tell your friends."

All afternoon he roamed the village, asking people what they knew about Seijuro, inviting them to the duel. "Come watch me fight Seijuro Sensei," he said to the innkeeper from whom he purchased an empty sake bottle, "tomorrow morning in the field on the north end of town."

The next morning Musashi rose well before dawn, paid his bill at the inn, and left for the field on the north end of town.

Seijuro, too, was busy readying himself. At his dojo, accompanied by his students, he checked his equipment. Carefully he inspected his sword, handling the blade with a polishing cloth. In a straight line before him, his students knelt, watching their master's every move. Seijuro sheathed his sword and tied it carefully to his belt. Bowing to his senior student, Seijuro appointed him his "second," his assistant, the man who would help end his life should he be mortally wounded.

When all was ready, he turned his attention to his students. "A duel is not a mere matter of fighting," he said to them. "It is a matter of honor. A true warrior meets an enemy with quiet courage. The way he conducts himself on the field of battle is the measure of his worth as an honorable human being." With those words, he strode out the door to meet Musashi.

Seijuro, followed by his second and his students, made his way across the village to the edge of town. The sun had been up for almost an hour. Seijuro figured that it was proper that the young upstart Musashi wait for him. As he rounded a corner and looked out over the field, he saw that a crowd had gathered.

"Musashi," he thought disgustedly. "He doesn't even have the decency to realize that a duel is not a circus." The crowd cheered Seijuro as he entered their midst. Seijuro raised his chin and tried to ignore them. He looked around. Musashi was nowhere to be seen.

"Where is he?" he whispered gruffly to his second, who had arranged the time and place.

"I don't know, Sensei," his second replied. "He said he would be here at sunrise."

"Well, I don't see him. Do you?" Seijuro's voice rose almost to a shout. His students took a few steps back. They all knew their teacher's anger far too well.

People in the crowd began to whisper between themselves. A laugh rose from somewhere near the back. Seijuro's face was red with anger.

"I'm not waiting for some young upstart who thinks he can arrive anytime he wants to," Seijuro bellowed. "He has insulted me by his tardiness." He turned to leave.

"Seijuro," a voice rose from the middle of the crowd. "Seijuro, where have you been? I've been here since before sunrise." A man swaggered forward, elbowing his way through the crowd, tossing aside an empty sake bottle. It was Musashi.

Seijuro turned to face him. Musashi's clothes were damp and wrinkled. In his belt was not a katana, but a bokken, a wooden practice sword.

"Sorry about the mess," Musashi said, brushing some dry grass from his lapel. I didn't want to miss the fight, so I slept out here last night." He tucked a loose strand of hair behind his ear and grinned. "You ready?"

Seijuro's eyes flared with anger. "You insult me with your dirty clothes and your poor attitude."

"Then perhaps you would like to challenge me to a duel," Musashi replied, still grinning.

"Back up," Seijuro ordered the crowd, swinging his arm in a wide arc. "Back up, I said!"

Musashi moved in close, his hand on the handle of his bokken. His eyes were calm, steady. The noise of the crowd seemed to drop away as Musashi brought his mind to focus on Seijuro and Seijuro alone.

With a roar Seijuro drew his sword. The anger shot from his eyes. Musashi saw that his plan had worked. Seijuro had let his anger get the best of him. His anger was making him tense, and his tenseness was making him slow. That small decrease in speed would give Musashi the edge he needed. He drew his bokken. Seijuro sliced at him furiously. Musashi slipped the attack and brought his bokken up under the older man's chin. The wood cracked into his jaw, and the great Seijuro fell to the ground.

Musashi checked to make sure his opponent would not soon rise. He slid his bokken into his belt and brushed the dust and grass from his clothes. He bowed deeply, bowed politely to Seijuro's second, and bowed again to his students. He straightened his shoulders and walked with dignity through the crowd.

According to legend, Hisamori Takenouchi founded the martial art of jujitsu. He was a samurai master of the bokken (wooden sword) and the jo (short staff). Before founding the first known jujitsu school in 1532, he was a soldier, serving a daimyō (lord) in feudal Japan.

The Gentle Way of Jujitsu

Takenouchi lay on the now-quiet battlefield, drifting in and out of consciousness. All around him wounded soldiers moaned in pain. A dead samurai lay mere inches from his face. Takenouchi's shoulder throbbed, and his head pounded. Blood streamed down his face.

He knew that if he stayed on the battlefield much longer he could be killed by wild animals or by treasure hunters picking through the casualties for something of value. He struggled to his feet, fighting the nausea that washed over him in waves. If he could make it to the forest, he could hide in the underbrush. He might even find some moss to stop the bleeding in his shoulder when he removed the arrow sticking out of it.

Moving carefully around bodies of men and horses, Takenouchi made his way to the edge of the field. Blood and pain clouded his vision. Just a few more feet, and he would be under cover. Just a few more feet.

Takenouchi awoke. He was lying on a mat covered by warm animal skins. An old man squatted by an open fire, stirring something in a large pot.

"Where am I?" Takenouchi asked.

"You're awake," said the old man. He stood and went to Takenouchi's mat in the corner of the room. "How do you feel?"

"Well enough, considering the injuries," Takenouchi replied, trying to sit. The room went dark for a moment, and he fell back onto the mat.

"Rest," the old man said. "Your head is healing. Somebody clubbed you pretty hard. And you lost a lot of blood when I removed the arrow from your shoulder. All day yesterday, I thought I was going to lose you."

Takenouchi reached up to where the arrow had been. A thick bandage covered the spot. "You removed it?" he asked.

"Yes," said the old man. "I've fought my share of battles. I know a thing or two about treating injuries like yours." He returned to his pot and spooned a dark liquid into a bowl. "Drink this," he said. "You need to rebuild your blood."

Takenouchi gingerly propped himself up and accepted the bowl. He tasted the dark liquid. It was faintly bitter but warm and comforting.

"You can call me Sato," said the old man. "This is my house, and you are welcome to it."

"My name is Takenouchi." He looked around. Sato's house was tiny, a single room, barely enough space for a couple of sleeping mats and a cooking fire. "Do you live here alone?" he asked. "It's a long way to the nearest town."

"Alone?" the old man said. "Yes, in a way I guess you could say I live here alone." He took a tattered cape from a hook and wrapped it around his shoulders. "But I like to think that I live with the trees, and the sky, and the animals. And occasionally a visitor like you. I meditate, I do some exercises, and I live off what the forest and my garden provide. It's a good life."

"But you were a soldier, a samurai?"

"I was," Sato said. "Until I tired of the killing." A look crossed the old man's face, a look Takenouchi had seen on old soldiers before, a look of both strength and deep sadness. Takenouchi's mind wandered to the battlefield he had just left. He understood how the old man felt.

Days passed, then weeks. Each day, Takenouchi spent more and more time working in Sato's garden and walking in the forest that surrounded his house. Gradually his strength returned. The pain in his head eased.

One day while walking, he found a long, straight oak branch. He cut it down and brought it back to Sato's cottage. Sitting cross-legged beside the garden, he whittled away the excess until he had a bokken, a wooden practice sword. Carefully, he checked the balance and then smoothed the surface by rubbing it with sand. That night he slept with his weapon beside his mat the way that soldiers usually did.

The next morning, cautiously at first, Takenouchi began his practice. His shoulder ached, but the ache was an old pain, the pain of a limb that was healing, not the pain of a limb being newly injured. He found an old tree stump and dropped a stroke down onto its center. He had a lot of work to do to build the strength in that arm again. A soldier with a weak side didn't last long in battle.

After several weeks of training, Takenouchi's shoulder was nearly back to normal. His headaches were almost gone, and he decided it was time to go back to work. He approached Sato in his garden.

"I think the time has come for me to leave," he said. He felt a lump in his throat. He had grown very fond of the old man.

"Will you go back to being a soldier?" Sato asked.

"It is what I do," Takenouchi replied.

"You will go back to killing and possibly being killed yourself?"

"It is what a soldier does."

"Then may I ask something from you, as a soldier, before you leave?"

"Certainly," Takenouchi said, bowing to his old friend. "Anything. I owe you my life."

"Attack me," said Sato stepping out of the garden.

"What do you mean?"

"Attack me. Try to grab me. As a favor."

Takenouchi didn't understand, but as a favor to Sato, he walked up and tried to grab his arm.

"No, no," Sato said, "Attack me."

Takenouchi lunged for the man's throat. But before he could grasp it, he felt his wrist being brushed away. His elbow locked out. His arm cranked over his head. Not sure what happened, Takenouchi picked himself up from the dust.

"Attack me," Sato commanded again.

This time Takenouchi rushed him. Sato could obviously take care of himself. Takenouchi ducked low, thinking to knock the man over. But in midstride, he felt Sato's foot knock his own feet out from under him. A quick twist of Sato's hips propelled the young samurai again into the dust. Takenouchi scrambled to his feet and grabbed for his bokken. Sato stood calmly waiting for him. Takenouchi swung the sword, thinking to thump the old man on the head. But Sato was quickly inside the swing, locking up Takenouchi's arms and stripping the sword from his hands.

"Are you hurt?" Sato asked.

"No," said Takenouchi. "Of course not."

"But had you attacked a superior foe like that in battle, would you be hurt?"

"Hurt, or dead," replied Takenouchi.

"But I was able to stop you without hurting you," Sato pointed out.

"Yes." Takenouchi wasn't sure what Sato's point might be.

"Come, sit," said the old man walking to the doorway of his cottage. "Let me tell you what I have learned here in the forest these many years. A soldier sees an attack and says, 'I must kill or be killed.' I see an attack and I know that I must keep it from hurting me. But whether I choose to kill or even hurt my attacker is up to me."

Takenouchi sat for a moment, taking in what Sato had said.

"You don't have to kill," Sato said. "If you know how to take your attacker's center, each time, every time, you can keep yourself safe. Then you can choose to kill or not kill."

"Can you teach me?" Takenouchi asked.

"I was hoping you'd ask," the old man rose and headed back to his garden. "First, help me bring in enough cabbage for our supper."

The challenge match has a long history in Japan. As they progressed, some kenjutsu students would go on Musha shugyō, a warrior's pilgrimage, traveling the country, challenging swordsmen to duels. Some were searching for a worthy teacher to take them to the next level. Others were auditioning for a job as a bodyguard or soldier. Many just wanted to make a name for themselves. Because duels are illegal in most modern countries, challenge matches have fallen out of favor. Masters who still take challenges often have their own rules and customs for doing so.

A Sword Match Unlike Any Other

It was deadly cold already, and the sun wasn't even down yet. Bob sipped his coffee slowly. Once he was finished with it, the restaurant staff would throw him out. Even fast food joints had a limited tolerance for homeless folks taking up space in their dining room. Bob wasn't sure what to do next. All the shelters were full. He had spent his last nickel on the coffee, so he couldn't afford a bus ticket. And word on the street was that tonight the weather might dip down to 20 degrees below zero, and it would be even colder with the wind chill. Bob glanced up at the counter help. They were keeping an eye on him.

A couple of college kids slid into the booth across from him.

"So you're saying that your teacher will take any challenge from anyone who comes through the door?"

"Yup," the other kid said. "Any student of the sword can come in and make a challenge."

"Then what?"

"Then it's usually over pretty quickly."

"Because he cuts off their head?"

"Don't be ridiculous. We use bokken, wooden swords, so there's no cutting. A few bruises, sometimes a broken bone, but usually nothing too serious. If you win—not that you're likely to win; nobody has yet—you're invited to teach a class. If you lose, sensei will feed you, let you stay at the dojo if you're from out of town and don't have a room, and then you go home with more experience than you had when you issued the challenge."

"So if I wanted to go in and challenge your sensei, I'd just walk up to him and say, 'let's fight?'"

"No, there's etiquette. So if I wanted to challenge him, which I wouldn't because I'm his student, but if I did want to challenge him, I would go up to him, bow, and say, 'Sensei, my name is Todd Berquist. I am a student of White Crane style, and I wish a lesson.'"

"That takes guts, to do what your sensei is doing, to take on all comers like that."

"Sensei has no shortage of guts. That's part of the reason I'm training with him."

The kid looked at his phone. "6:15. I had better get to work, and you have class, don't you?"

"It's just two doors down, so I have a couple of minutes."

Bob stared into his coffee. So this teacher would give him a meal and a warm place to sleep just for losing a sword fight? That might be the answer to his problem. It sounded a bit frightening. Bob had never fought with a sword in his life. But just sleeping on the street in the dead of winter was frightening. A friend of his had died last week. He was in his thirties, homeless like Bob. He just lay down on a cold sidewalk, the temperature dropped, and he never woke up. Bob knew that if he didn't get a roof over his head, he too could be dead of exposure before morning. The college kid threw away his trash and headed out the door. Bob followed him.

The dojo was warm and brightly lit. All the students took off their shoes and boots when they entered, so Bob did too, bending over the end of his sock so nobody could see the hole where his big toe was. He turned to one of the students.

"Which one is Sensei?" he asked. The student pointed to a middle-aged man in a white jacket and something that looked like really baggy, really long, black culottes. Bob took a deep breath, stuffed his mittens and hat into his jacket pockets. He walked up to the man, and made an awkward bow.

"My name is Bob Carlson. I am a student of, um, Black Dog. I wish a lesson."

Sensei had seen the man come in. He was wearing jeans and a parka that was a size too small. His greasy hair was tied back with a shoe lace. Sensei would have jumped to the conclusion that the man was homeless and living on the streets if it hadn't been for some of the other students of the sword who had come through his door. Some of them had been on *musha shugyō*, a warrior's pilgrimage. They were living on almost nothing, and they came in here looking like a ragbag. Sensei had found that you couldn't judge skill by the cut of a person's clothes. But this guy? This guy really did look like a street person.

Sensei bowed back. "Black Dog," he said. "I haven't heard of that style."

"Um, I'm not from around here," Bob said.

"Where are you from?" Sensei asked.

"Oh, these days, just here and there, sometimes it seems like nowhere."

"*Musha shugyō?*" Sensei asked. Bob's face was blank. "Warrior's pilgrimage?"

"Yes, of course," Bob said. "Something like that."

"Do you have your weapons?" Sensei asked.

Bob felt his stomach sink. He knew there would be a catch. He couldn't just come in without a sword and pretend to be some kind of sword master. "No," Bob said. "Uh, the airline, you know, wouldn't let me fly with them. I thought maybe, uh, I could borrow something."

"Of course," Sensei replied. He motioned for one of the students to bring a bokken. "You can hang your jacket on one of the hooks."

Bob pulled off his jacket. Then he took off one of his flannel shirts, then the other. He was left with a t-shirt over a long-sleeved undershirt with a hole in the elbow. Since everyone else seemed to be barefoot, he pulled off his socks and cringed a little bit at the smell as he stuffed them in his jacket pocket. He couldn't imagine this was going to work. Any minute now they would see him for the impostor he was. But, on the other hand, it was cold. He needed shelter and was out of options. All he really had to do was to get into the duel and then lose. How hard could that be?

Sensei stepped onto deck, bowed to kamiza, and called for the students to move off deck.

Bob picked up the bokken, bowed at the edge of the deck like Sensei had done.

Sensei faced off and bowed to Bob. He was having a terrible time reading this man's body language. Bob looked to be maybe 40 or 45, fit, lean, strong but not muscle-bound. That was typical for someone who trained in the sword. Maybe he really was a sword adept and not just some bum. Sensei took up a chudan stance, his sword pointed at Bob's throat level.

Bob wasn't sure what to do. There was something in Sensei's stance that made the blood stop in his veins. Maybe it was the point of that wooden sword aimed right at his throat. Maybe it was the intensity in Sensei's eyes. But again, what did he have to lose? No matter how dangerous Sensei was, the weather was worse. Bob thought about mirroring Sensei's stance. But if he did, it might look like resistance. If he offered resistance, Sensei would just have to power through it to defeat him. Bob decided to just stand there and make himself as easy a target as possible.

Sensei assessed Bob's stance. It was a natural one, feet shoulder width apart. The sword was low, kind of like a gedan stance but much more relaxed. Bob's face was blank. Sensei was used to being able to read an opponent's intent long before they struck, but this man was blank. He must be more experienced than I thought, Sensei thought to himself. Only a master could mask his thoughts so completely.

Bob wondered what Sensei was waiting for. He stood there motionless, sword at the ready, not doing anything. *What does a guy have to do to get beat around here?* he thought. *Look, no resistance. Nothing, OK?*

Sensei moved a bit to his right. Bob just squared up so he was facing him again. Sensei had never seen that kind of economy of motion. Bob had to be from one of the naturalistic styles, and probably pretty experienced at that. His body was no more tense than a man waiting for a bus. How could he be so calm knowing that an attack could come at any moment?

Bob waited.

Sensei waited.

Bob waited.

Sensei waited. Finally, Sensei knew that he had to do something. This strange master would probably humiliate him. Nobody left that large an opening unless it was a trap. But he had to do something. All his students were watching. He had to attack. Sensei stepped forward.

But just then, at the very same moment Sensei moved forward, Bob took a step back. He dropped his bokken and put his hands up. "I give up," he said. "I'm not a sword guy. I'm just hungry."

Sensei dropped the tip of his sword down to gedan stance. He wasn't completely sure this wasn't some kind of new tactic.

"I'm just a homeless guy," Bob said. "I wanted someplace warm to sleep. It's going to be wicked cold tonight, and I heard you sometimes let sword guys stay here overnight. And I'm really sorry…" Bob paused. Sensei had shifted his sword to his left hand and was holding out his right. Bob took it and shook it.

Sensei's whole world suddenly rearranged itself. He realized how all through the duel he had been fighting his imagination. This man who had seconds ago been a master was now a homeless person, but more than that, this homeless person was suddenly a human being. He was human, and the weather was cold. That was the most real part of this whole experience.

"Thank you for the lesson," Sensei said to Bob, bowing to him deeply. "I have a sandwich and a couch in my office. You are welcome to both."

Gichin Funakoshi is best known as the man who brought Okinawan karate to Japan. The style he founded there has become known as Shotokan karate. Funakoshi was a small man, but physically strong from his karate training and mentally strong from his studies. It is because of those strengths and his remarkable self-control that he was chosen over men much more powerful than he was to bring karate to Japan.

Karate Master Gichin Funakoshi Learns Great Power and Great Control

Funakoshi wrestled with the tatami mat he was carrying. The long, narrow straw mat was several inches taller than he was and awkward to carry. When the storm blew against it, the mat bent like a bow. When the wind let up a little or changed direction, the mat sprang straight again, throwing Funakoshi off balance. It was going to be tricky getting the mat onto the roof. Especially tricky given that the rain seemed to be picking up, too.

"Funakoshi-san," a neighbor shouted over the howl of the wind. "What are you doing? Are you having trouble with your roof? Is it leaking? Maybe you should just let it leak. It's not safe to be up patching your roof with a typhoon blowing in."

"The roof is fine, Hanasato-san. Thank you for asking," Funakoshi called back. He laid the tatami flat against the tile of the roof and scrambled the rest of the way up.

"If the roof is fine, what are you doing up there in your underwear?" Hanasato shouted.

"Just a little exercise," Funakoshi grinned at his neighbor who was squinting over the side fence, trying to keep the blowing rain out of his eyes.

"Is it one of those martial arts things?" Hanasato asked.

"I suppose it is," Funakoshi said.

Hanasato shook his head. "Does your wife know you're up there?" he called.

"Oh, yes," Funakoshi answered. "She's inside, though."

"Most sane people are," Hanasato replied. "Do be careful." He pulled his jacket more closely around him and trotted back to his house.

Funakoshi climbed to the peak of the house. From there he could see that the sky had turned a sickly shade of gray-green. A branch blew off a nearby tree and struck him in the chest. He looked down. No blood but a large red mark. The wind blew hard against his face, making it difficult for him to catch his breath.

Stability, he told himself, is partly a matter of body, but partly a matter of mind. If a man thinks he will fall over, he will. Slowly, carefully, Funakoshi bent over and picked up the tatami. The wind tugged at it, trying to rip it from his grasp, but Funakoshi held tight, bringing it up edge on to the wind. He took a solid horse straddle stance and turned the tatami flat to the wind.

The wind caught the tatami and lifted Funakoshi up off the roof. His feet scrambled against the wet tiles, trying to find footing, but the wind was in control. A powerful gust grabbed him and threw him off the end of the roof. He landed in the mud, the tatami on top of him.

"Are you all right?" his wife called from the door.

"I'm fine," Funakoshi answered, standing. "I just need to take a stronger stance before I tip up the tatami."

"Come inside," his wife shouted.

"In a minute," Funakoshi replied. "I know what I'm doing."

The door to the house closed, and Funakoshi tucked the tatami under his arm and started up the ladder. It was a matter of using the strength of the stance, he thought to himself. He needed to stand sideways to the wind.

Funakoshi squinted against the wet sand, branches, and other debris that beat against him. The wind was picking up. He would have to go inside soon. He took a low stance on the peak of the roof, spread his feet wide apart, tightened his leg muscles, pictured himself gripping the roof with the center of his body. When the straddle stance was the best he could make it, he flipped the tatami up. The wind hit it hard. Funakoshi stutter-stepped back, then caught his balance again. The force blew the tatami hard against his shoulder. The top of it flapped stiffly against his face. Slowly, his muscles straining, he pushed the mat away from him, then let the wind push it back. Again he pushed it away from him, tightening his legs against the force, forcing his arms to hold against the raw power of the wind and rain.

Gradually, still holding against the wind, he shifted his stance—front, back, straddle stance again. His body strained. He fought to keep his mind focused. Slowly, he lowered the mat to the roof. It was a mess, covered with mud, bent and broken in places. Funakoshi smiled to himself. He wondered if he looked that bad. Carefully he climbed down off the roof and entered the house, dripping and cold.

His wife met him at the door with a towel. He wiped off the mud and debris before stepping up onto the tatami floor of the living room.

"Was it worth it?" his wife asked, an amused look in her eye.

"Oh, yes," he replied. "Most definitely."

Funakoshi dropped his books and shoes inside the front door of his house. On the way to the closet, he stripped off his uniform. Hanging it carefully in the closet, he put on his good kimono and checked his hair in the mirror. The school where he taught was out for the day. His wife and children were already at her parents' house, and he wanted to get there in time for dinner. Quickly he snatched up a couple of small cakes to offer at the family altar when he got there. It was a two-mile walk, and he didn't have time to waste.

After a day in the classroom, he enjoyed the late afternoon air. The road to his in-laws' village took him through pine groves and farmland. He breathed in the smell of the trees and the crops. The cool breeze felt good against his face. It would be good to see his father-in-law again.

A rustle in the bushes brought Funakoshi out of his thoughts. Out of the corner of his eye, he saw three shapes half-hidden behind the trees of a small pine grove. Keeping his eyes forward, he continued to walk. Behind him he heard the sound of footsteps on gravel. He stopped and turned around. Behind him stood two men. A third was making his way out of the woods. All three had towels tied over their faces.

Funakoshi stood quietly assessing the situation. They didn't move like martial artists. They didn't seem to be trying to surround him. He guessed that they were thugs, not trained fighters. He could probably handle all three if it came to that.

"What's wrong?" one of the thugs said loudly, approaching Funakoshi with a swagger. "Don't you have any manners? The least you could do is wish us a good evening."

"Good evening," Funakoshi said simply.

"That's 'Good evening, sir,'" the other thug said.

"Good evening, sir," Funakoshi repeated.

"Kind of scrawny," the first thug said, loudly. "He isn't going to be much of a challenge." The other two laughed.

"I'm sorry, sir," Funakoshi said politely. "I think you've mistaken me for someone else. I'm not looking for a fight. I'm just traveling to my in-laws' house in Mawashi. So if you'll . . ."

"Shut up," the largest of the three commanded. He picked up a stick that was lying beside the road and slapped it into his other hand. "I ought to beat you over the head just because I find your voice so annoying."

"You could do that," Funakoshi answered. "But it wouldn't prove anything. As you've pointed out, I'm a lot smaller than you. You have a stick. I don't . . ."

"So you're saying you're a coward, that you don't want to fight."

"Why should I fight a fight with such lopsided odds?" Funakoshi replied.

"Never mind the fight," said the loud one. "He's not worth it."

"Just give us your money," said the big one, poking Funakoshi in the chest with the stick.

"Terribly sorry," Funakoshi replied, turning the large pocket in his sleeve inside out. "I don't have any money."

"Figures," said the loud one. "Then give us some tobacco."

"Sorry," Funakoshi said. "I don't smoke."

"No money, no tobacco. Looks like we're going to have to beat you up after all." The big thug took a step forward, slapping his stick into his hand.

"Perhaps you'd consider taking these, instead." Funakoshi held up the small sack he was carrying. The loud thug snatched it out of his hands and peered inside.

"Cakes," he grumbled. "Is that all?"

"Yes, I'm afraid that's all."

"Well, I'm feeling generous," said the loud one. "Get lost, squirt. We'll wait until next time to beat you up."

Funakoshi sat with Itosu, his teacher, the next night. They sipped tea together and Funakoshi told him about the thugs he had faced on his way to Mawashi.

"You found a way not to hurt them," Itosu nodded approvingly. "Good. Very good."

Funakoshi lowered his head modestly. But inside he was beaming at his teacher's praise.

"But you lost your cakes," Itosu observed. "What did you offer at your in-laws' altar?"

"A heartfelt prayer," Funakoshi answered smiling. His teacher laughed.

"I think you offered your wife's family something much more valuable than cakes," he said, pouring Funakoshi another cup of tea. "You offered them the knowledge that their daughter is married to a good man, one who can protect her if he has to, but who can control himself and his temper even when challenged."

Funakoshi sipped the tea and smiled.

*M*orihei Ueshiba was the founder of the Japanese art of aikido. As a young man, he studied jujitsu, as well as sword and spear techniques. While in the Japanese army he was certified to teach combat arts to soldiers. Later in his life, however, he decided that attacking another person, even for a good reason, upsets the harmony of the universe. He developed aikido, which is a completely defensive art. Aikido students refer to Ueshiba as Osensei, which means "honored teacher."

The Strange Disappearance of Aikido Master Morihei Ueshiba

Morihei Ueshiba was a man of rare abilities. One day during a demonstration he asked five American military police officers to hold him down, to restrain him as they would restrain a dangerous criminal. The police officers surrounded Ueshiba Osensei. Five young, strong soldiers latched onto the small, eighty-year-old man. One by one, the police officers were tossed off the pile like rag dolls until Ueshiba Osensei was able to stroll through the midst of them completely free. The people who observed the demonstration say he wasn't even breathing hard.

Another time during a demonstration he defended himself unarmed against a sword master with a bokken, a wooden sword. The man could easily have knocked out or even killed a lesser opponent. But Ueshiba Osensei seemed able to read the sword master's mind. He ducked and dodged, smoothly, easily. The sword master used his most effective techniques against Ueshiba Osensei, but was unable to touch him. Later Ueshiba Osensei said that he could see the path the sword would take before it even moved. The path appeared to him like trails of light in the air. All he had to do was stay outside the trails.

These demonstrations were remarkable, without a doubt. But perhaps more remarkable, and perhaps more unbelievable, was the time Ueshiba Osensei vanished into thin air.

Ueshiba Osensei was talking with several of his students at home one evening. The students were talking about the mysterious powers of the ninja.

"It is said," a student remarked, "that a ninja can climb straight up the side of a building without ropes or ladders. Surely that takes mysterious powers."

"That's not so mysterious," said another. "They have claws they strap to their hands and feet. The claws dig into the wood or the mortar between the bricks. A ninja climbing a building is no more mysterious than a cat climbing a tree."

"But what about their invisibility?" said the first student. "How do you explain that?"

"Camouflage," said the second student. "Black clothes at night, green clothes for hiding in trees, white clothes for hiding in snow. The army does the same thing."

"But what about their ability to disappear?"

"Like I said, camouflage," said the second.

"No I mean to really disappear, to vanish into thin air," said the first.

"That," said the second, "is not possible."

"Mmm," said Ueshiba Osensei, who had been listening in on the conversation. The students' heads all turned to look at their sensei.

"It isn't," said the student. "It isn't possible. People don't just disappear."

"You're quick to label something impossible," Ueshiba Osensei said. "Have you tried it?"

"No," said the student, a little less sure of himself now.

"Do you know anyone who has spent years of his life trying to learn how to do it?"

"No." The student began to squirm.

"I see," Ueshiba Osensei said. "But still you believe it is impossible?"

The student was silent.

Ueshiba Osensei stood gracefully, then walked to an open place on the floor. "Come," he said to the student. "Come." He motioned for the rest of the students to stand and join him.

The students stood and faced their teacher.

"Attack me, all of you at once," Ueshiba Osensei commanded.

The students knew what their teacher was asking. They had attacked many times as a group on the training floor. It didn't seem to make a difference to Ueshiba Osensei whether he was attacked by one person or by a mob; he always managed to throw off his attackers and free himself. The students looked around at the furniture, trying to gauge whether they had room to roll out of the throws Osensei would be doing.

"Attack me," Osensei said again.

The students converged, each trying to grab a wrist, or a shoulder, or a lapel. They came together on all sides of their teacher, a large, teeming mass of hands reaching out for the grab.

Slowly, steadily, the students stepped back from the group. They looked around. All they saw were other students. Osensei was nowhere to be seen.

"So," they heard the voice from the top of the stairs. "So," Osensei said, "do you still believe it's impossible?"

The students tripped over each other to get to the base of the stairs. Looking up they saw their teacher sitting casually at the top.

"How?" asked several students at once.

"Can you teach us?" asked another. Heads nodded throughout the group.

"It's a matter of the proper use of qi, or energy," Osensei said descending the stairs. "Once you've developed your qi to a sufficient degree, no explanation will be necessary. Until that time, no explanation will be sufficient."

"Would you do it again?" a student asked.

"Am I a circus act?" Osensei asked. "No, these things take a great deal of energy. I won't expend that kind of energy just to satisfy your curiosity."

The students were silent.

"Maybe some other time," Osensei said with a smile. "Right now it's time for me to disappear into my bed for a good night's sleep. I suggest you do the same."

"The Empty Cup" is a traditional Zen parable that some believe tells the story of a real-life event from eighth-century China. In the real-life story the Zen Master Ryutan overfills the cup of Tokusan, a famous scholar, who came to Ryutan full of knowledge and opinions. In this tale, a karate teacher uses the parable to teach her new student a valuable lesson.

The Empty Cup

"I already have a lot of experience in the martial arts," Emma explained to her new sensei. "My Dad's in the Army, and he taught me some of their hand-to-hand combat. And then I studied with a Taekwondo teacher in the last city we lived in and a jujitsu teacher in the city before that. I can probably start studying brown belt material pretty soon, once I memorize the new stuff."

"I see," her sensei replied. "Why don't I take a look at how you move before we decide where you fit in the rank structure?"

"Sure," Emma said. "Do you want me to do some forms for you?"

"Let's do class first," Sensei said.

"Sure," Emma said, heading into the dressing room to change. She pulled her blue dobok out of her gym bag. Her mom had offered to buy her a white gi like the other students wore, but the blue dobok had such good memories. At her previous school, only members of the demonstration team could wear blue. When Emma earned this dobok, it was the proudest day of her life. She tied on her green belt and strode out onto the deck feeling like a bright flower growing up in the middle of a field of white snow.

"Line up," Sensei called. The students quickly found their places. Emma spotted a green belt and fell into line ahead of him. Sensei glanced at her and smiled slightly.

They bowed in, did some warm-ups, and then started some kick practice. Emma was sure that once Sensei saw her kicks, she would quickly promote her to an intermediate rank, maybe even brown belt. The other students around her were doing strange thrusting kicks, lower abdomen height, solar plexus height, some of them even knee height. Emma snapped out a fast front kick as high as she could throw it, head high, maybe even higher. Sensei watched and smiled slightly.

"I could *teach* kicks around here," Emma thought to herself. Sensei was up front showing how to kick into the back of a knee using a front kick. Emma remembered the master at her previous school. He could jump so high that sometimes he would have to kick down just to hit someone in the head. The group split up to kick the heavy bags, three to a bag. The rest of the students were kicking knee high. Emma tried a low kick but decided it didn't feel nearly as good as the high kicks and went back to kicking as high as she could. She was striking the bag right at the top. Maybe she could talk to Sensei about hanging at least one of the bags higher, so she could stretch herself.

The class then split by rank. Sensei put Emma with the white belts. Emma was disappointed. When the assistant instructor started showing them the first form, she was even more disappointed. It was exactly like the first form at her old school. She had learned that form a year ago. As she followed along with the group, she began looking around at the rest of the class to see if she knew any of the other forms as well. The form the yellow belts were doing was similar to a Taekwondo form. Maybe the blue belt one was, too.

"Emma," the assistant instructor brought her out of her speculation. "You're doing the turn wrong. Watch me." He punched and then brought his foot around in front of himself to make the turn into a low block.

"We used to turn like this at my old school," Emma said, punching and then bringing her foot behind herself before throwing the low block.

"A lot of schools do it that way," the assistant said. "We don't. Let me show you again how we do it."

Emma couldn't help but think that this way wasn't nearly as nice as her old way. Her way had more power, more flash. Maybe she'd talk to Sensei and show her the new way. Maybe they would change the form once they saw the advantages of doing a cross-behind turn.

After an hour, the class ended, and Emma was in a great mood. This new style wasn't as good as her old one, of course. But the people were nice, and Emma found she knew more than she thought, so it wouldn't take her long to advance.

When Sensei asked her into her office, Emma was sure it was to tell her what her new rank would be.

"Have a seat," Sensei motioned to a one of two chairs beside a table. "I can see you have worked hard in your old style."

"Thank you, Sensei," Emma replied.

"Tea?" Sensei asked. Emma nodded. Sensei brought out a couple of small tea cups and a pot of tea she had been steeping. She set a cup in front of Emma.

"Do you like our style of karate?" Sensei asked. Emma nodded again. They could talk about the changes Emma want to make to the style later.

Sensei began to pour the tea into Emma's cup. She poured until the cup was full. "Tea?" she asked again. Emma wasn't sure what she meant. Sensei then began to pour again. The cup overflowed. Tea spilled out onto the table, but still Sensei kept pouring.

"Stop," Emma said, getting up so the tea wouldn't spill over onto her lap. "Stop."

Sensei stopped pouring. "What's wrong?" she said.

Emma looked at her, not sure how to answer the question. Finally, she answered, "The tea cup was already full."

"Yes, it was," Sensei replied. "And so were you." Emma sat back down.

"From the moment you walked through the front door of the dojo, you have been full of knowledge from your old school. It's good knowledge. I can tell your teachers have taught you well. But you are so full of old knowledge that you have no room for new knowledge."

"Empty your cup, Emma, and I'll give you more tea."

Masutatsu (Mas) Oyama is the founder of Kyokushinkai Karate. When he was a boy, he studied the Eighteen Hands, a Chinese martial art. At age fifteen, he left Korea, where he had been born, and China, where he had grown up, for Japan. He wanted to become a fighter pilot and test his courage serving in World War II. But the war ended before he could sign up, and Mas Oyama turned to the martial arts to provide him with the challenges he sought.

Why Karate Master Mas Oyama Shaved His Head Twice

Mas knew that most of his friends thought he was crazy. They all gathered at a local Tokyo restaurant to see him off.

"I like the haircut, Mas," one of his friends commented. "It makes you look like an egg."

"Yeah, what's going on, Mas?" another taunted. "Don't the mountain spirits like hair?"

Mas ran his hand over his smooth scalp. It felt strange but good. It felt good like a fresh beginning feels good.

"Well, boys," he said, taking another sip of his drink. "I've decided that if I'm going to train, I'm going to do it right. I'm not going to come down from that mountain until my hair reaches my shoulders. I figure it'll take about a year, maybe two. When you next see me, I'll be a new man."

"Well, certainly a hairier one, I hope. You really don't have the head to make baldness look good." The friend raised his glass in a salute.

Mas's friends laughed. But they knew better than to underestimate Mas's willpower. If he said he would be up there for a year, he would do it.

Mas dropped his pack in the center of a small grove of trees. The sound of a waterfall roared and splashed just over the hill. The smell of damp moss filled the air. The cool, spring breeze felt good on his bare scalp.

Stripping off his jacket, he scanned the grove until he found a tree about three inches thick. Taking a solid stance he faced the tree, then swinging his hips, he whipped his leg into a powerful round kick. His shin landed on the tree trunk with a thud. The pain spread like a fire up Mas's shin.

"I have some serious conditioning to do," he said to himself as he prepared for a second kick.

The waterfall had ceased to be painfully cold. It was now only bone-chillingly, muscle-numbingly cold. But deep in his belly, Mas could feel the powerful core of warmth as he rose from his morning meditation. The sun was beginning to come up as Mas stood, the icy water still streaming down from the rocks above onto his head and shoulders.

"It's going to be hot today," he said running a hand through his bushy short hair. Hot days were good. They could be just as good a test as cold.

Finding a spot where the water from the waterfall beat down hardest, Mas took a strong stance in the knee-deep water and began his body-hardening exercises. His feet tight and stable beneath him, he tightened his entire body and punched slowly, as though trying to push his fist through a huge pile of sand. Then relaxing completely, he pulled his fist back, tightened and punched again. One hundred times on the left side. One hundred times on the right side. Mas shifted his feet slightly and began working on his blocks.

The snow made the rock slippery. Mas's feet skidded out from under him and he fell to the ground. Rising, he stood again beside the waist-high boulder. Bending his knees deep, he sprang into the air. Again his feet reached the top of the rock, but slipped off the edge. Mas slid down the side of the rock and landed hard on his left hip. He stood, pushed the pain out of his mind, backed away from the rock, and took a few practice jumps. His short hair bounced on his forehead. What he needed to do was get his knees higher. Again he stood next to the rock, sprung, and this time landed squarely in the center of the rock. To make sure he had the technique, he tried again, and again landed squarely on the rock. A grin spread across his face. Hopping down, he began scanning the area for a larger boulder.

The fall leaves crackled under Mas's feet as he made his way to his punching rock. The path was familiar to him. Each day for a year and a half, he had made his way to the same spot. At first he had punched his hands into wet sand, then pebbles. Then he found a fallen log and used that for a few months. The skin on his knuckles and palm had hardened and calloused. The nerves had died. And Mas's hands, when formed into fists, had come to look like heavy clubs.

Tucking his hair behind his ears, Mas knelt before the smooth flat rock. He liked to think that if he looked hard enough, he could see the indentations where his fists had pounded over and over into the surface. Breathing, relaxing, he began striking the rock. Steadily he punched. Harder. Harder. Harder. Crackle. Mas stopped. In the center of the rock, a small crack had formed. Mas took a deep breath and punched. His fist broke the surface, and the rock split into two even pieces.

Standing, Mas made his way back along the path. He stopped at the clearing, tied his hair back in a ponytail, gathered his pack, and started down the mountain.

Mas and his friends stood on the edge of the ring, watching two fighters compete. The first All-Japan Karate Tournament looked as though it was going to be a resounding success. Karateka from all over Japan awaited their turn to compete. Mas ran his hand over his head. He had kept the long hair and had just oiled it and pulled it back for the tournament. His friends joked that it made him look like one of the old samurai. He figured he'd cut it soon. But somehow it just didn't seem time yet.

As Mas waited for his turn, he watched some of the most skillful karateka he'd ever seen. He was not the only one in the auditorium who was in good shape. He hoped his training would be enough.

From the front table, Mas heard his name being called. He reported to the front table and learned which ring he was to fight in. He reported to the ring and began his warm-up.

The official strode into the ring. Standing opposite his opponent, Mas bowed, and on signal took a fighting stance. The other fighter did so as well. Mas saw the hole in his defense immediately. Seizing the opportunity, he faked high, then punched hard to the man's solar plexus.

The man sagged, and Mas caught his chin with an uppercut. The fight was over mere seconds after it had started.

Mas's friends crowded around him, slapping him on the back.

"I think I blinked," Mas said.

"What?" a friend asked.

"I think I blinked, when I threw the uppercut, I might have had my eyes closed for a second. I shouldn't have closed my eyes."

"Who cares?" the friend said, slapping him on the back again. "It was a great uppercut. It was an incredible fight."

The crowd gathered around the mat where Mas was scheduled to fight his last fight. None of the opponents he had fought had lasted longer than a couple of minutes. Word had spread through the arena that a strong twenty-four-year-old fighter was defeating every opponent he fought. The ring where the final fight was to be held was surrounded by people eight or ten deep.

Mas stepped into the ring. He bowed to his opponent. He bowed to the referee. He took his fighting stance, and again immediately saw the opening. His opponent's defense was weak. He could blast right through it. When the man moved to attack, Mas hooked over his arm and punched him solidly in the chest. The man staggered back. Mas followed. His opponent tried to get his guard back up, but Mas punched through it, around it, past it, landing several short sharp blows to the man's ribs. The power knocked him over. On the floor, clutching his ribs, he tried to stand, but grimaced at the pain. The referee called the fight and declared Mas the winner.

"I think my concentration could have been better," Mas said to his friend later outside the arena.

"I don't see how," the friend answered. "It looked great to me."

"The focus was there," Mas said. "It was a good fight. I'm glad I won. All I'm saying it that I think I could have done better. There was something I should have learned out there on the mountain that I don't think I've gotten yet."

"Mas," his friend replied. "Stop worrying about it. Don't you understand that after this tournament, you'll have people from all over the country wanting to study with you? Even if it wasn't a perfect fight, it was still the best one at the tournament. You are the best fighter in the country."

"Maybe so," Mas replied.

"Definitely so," his friend replied. "Now, we have some celebrating to do. You're going to meet us at the restaurant in an hour, right?"

"Right," agreed Mas, running his fingers through his hair. "I'll meet you there. I have a few things to take care of first."

A small crowd gathered at the restaurant. Mas's friends were telling stories of how they had trained for their black belts together. Now and then they would shoot a glance at the door, wondering where Mas was. It wasn't like him to be late.

It was nearly nine o'clock when he finally came through the door. He sat down at the table and removed his cap.

"I like the haircut, Mas," a friend said. "It makes you look like an egg. You're going up the mountain again?"

Mas nodded. "One more time."

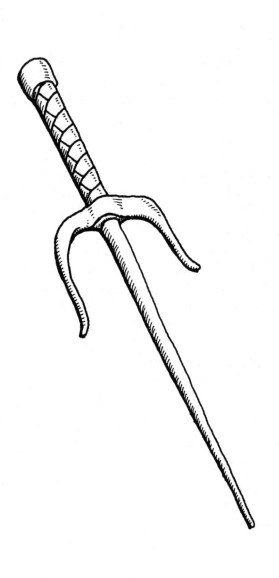

*C*hatan Yara grew up in the village of Chatan in Okinawa in the late eighteenth century. When he was a boy, his parents began considering what would be a good career for him. Because he was large for his age and strong, they sent him to China to learn martial arts. He lived there for twenty years, studying with Wong Chung-Yoh. When he returned to Okinawa he made his living as a Chinese translator, teaching martial arts in the evenings.

Though Yara studied bo and broadsword in China, when he returned to Okinawa, he began practicing with sai, the short-handled trident. Soon he achieved a reputation for being one of the finest sai artists in the country.

A Kobudo Master Takes on a Bright Young Man

Yara returned from his daily walk. In front of his house stood a young man holding a pair of sai. The young man's shoulders and chest were broad, and he was a good three inches taller than Yara, whom most people considered huge.

"Good afternoon, sir," the young man called to Yara. "Are you Chatan Yara?"

"I am," Yara replied.

"I am Shiroma," the young man said bowing deeply. "I am from the island of Hama Higa."

Yara glanced at the young man's sai. They were beautifully crafted, as were all the sai made on Hama Higa. But they were badly banged and rusted in places. Shiroma had obviously been using them much more than he had been caring for them. "What brings you to my home, Shiroma?" Yara asked.

"I am looking for a teacher," Shiroma replied. "I have heard you are one of the best. I am already a very capable sai fighter. Most of the teachers I've talked to couldn't teach me much. So I've come to you."

Yara smiled. The young man reminded him of himself when he was that age. He was strong, sure of himself, perhaps a little too sure of himself. He might make a good student, but Yara had no time for new students. His translating work and the students he already had kept him constantly busy.

"I'm sorry," Yara replied. "I only take students who have been referred to me."

"What kind of referral do I need? Perhaps I can get it."

"Please don't bother yourself," Yara replied. "I'm not taking new students at this time. Good afternoon." Yara turned to unlatch his front gate.

"Wait a minute!" the young man shouted, then realized he was shouting. "Pardon me," he said more quietly. "I haven't come all this way just to be told that you aren't taking students. Let me prove that I'm as good as I say I am."

"I'm not taking new students, even 'good' ones," Yara said patiently.

"Then why don't you prove to me how good you are?" The young man's eyes locked onto Yara's. Yara looked into them, and saw the challenge there. Perhaps this young buck needed at least a lesson in manners.

"All right," Yara said. "I will fight you. Meet me just before sunset on the top the hill just outside town."

The young man bowed again. "Thank you, sir," he said. "I have been working on sai technique and strategy all my life. I think you will find me a good challenge."

That evening, Yara walked slowly and steadily up the path to the top of the hill. He was typically able to spar with his young students without actually hurting them. His skill and size allowed him to dominate the fight, and his students rarely received more than bruises and sprains at his hands. But it would be difficult to fight someone as strong as Shiroma without seriously hurting him. Yara knew all too well how much damage a sai could cause. He hoped he wouldn't have to maim Shiroma to humble him.

When Yara crested the top of the hill, Shiroma was waiting for him. The beads of sweat on Shiroma's brow said that he had been practicing and warming up.

"Hello," Shiroma called. "I'm glad you're here."

Yara squinted into the sun to see Shiroma coming toward him. "Would you like some time to warm up?" Shiroma asked.

Yara shielded his eyes with his free hand. "No," he said. "I'm quite warm from the climb." He pulled his sai from their carrying bag, and took out a cloth to wipe the oil from them. His master had always taught him to respect and care for his weapons. He checked the surface and grip of his sai, then put away the cloth.

"Are you ready?" Shiroma asked. Yara nodded. The two bowed formally to each other. Shiroma transferred a sai to his left hand and flipped both blades open. Yara also transferred one sai, but kept his closed, the blades tight against his arms for blocking. The two circled, sizing each other up.

Gradually, Shiroma worked his way around Yara, positioning himself so the sun was at his back and in Yara's eyes. Yara quickly sidestepped, clearing his view. It was a time-honored strategy that Shiroma was using—take advantage of the sun to blind your attacker momentarily, then strike before his vision clears. Yara himself might have used such a strategy at that age. Shiroma faked high and tried to punch low, but Yara slipped the attack. Shiroma was punching hard, with all his muscles tight. Yara would have to block him hard, perhaps even break his arm just to stay safe.

Again Shiroma began circling. The strategy had worked for him in the past. He hoped it would work again. Yara squinted as the sun came into his field of vision. Shiroma smiled and shifted slightly so the sun was directly at his back. He saw Yara blink and took the opportunity to attack. Suddenly, everything went bright. A powerful flash filled his vision. Instinctively, he pulled his attack and tried to move backward out of range. But it was too late. He felt the cool point of Yara's sai at his throat.

"Enough," Shiroma said, blinking to clear his vision. "You win." Yara took a couple of steps back and bowed.

"What happened?" Shiroma asked.

Yara held up a sai. It caught the light of the setting sun. Yara directed the reflection first onto Shiroma's chest, then up into his eyes.

Shiroma bowed. "I'll be leaving now."

"I think that's a good idea," Yara replied. "Thank you for the fight."

"Thank you for the lesson," Shiroma said. "I see I still have a few things to learn."

Yara nodded. "For example, this evening, don't forget to clean your sai."

The Sengoku period of Japan (c. 1467–c. 1600) is sometimes known as the Age of Warring States. Daimyōs, feudal lords who ruled particular regions of the country, fought each other for territory and for influence over the Shogun, the military dictator of Japan. Each daimyō had his own samurai warriors, who served as bodyguards and foot soldiers. Samurai Shibata Katsuie served Oda Nobunaga, one of the most powerful daimyōs of the era.

Samurai Warrior Shibata and the Siege of Chokoji Castle

Shibata Katsuie was a samurai. His whole life was given over to serving the Oda clan of 16th century Japan. His skills and warrior spirit were unmatched. Once Shibata set his mind on victory, nothing but death could turn him aside.

That's why in 1567, his lord, Oda Nobunaga, put him in charge of the army and gave him orders to invade a neighboring province and crush an alliance that was threatening the Oda clan. Shibata triumphed, and Oda made him head of the army. Under Shibata's leadership the Oda samurai became a fearsome force.

One day, Oda Nobunaga called Shibata into his presence.

"Our enemies Asai and Asakura have become too strong," Oda said. "They endanger our clan and must be beaten back."

"Command me," Shibata said, "and I will destroy them and any other enemy that threatens you."

"That's not what I need from you," Oda replied. "I myself will take the army out to meet Asai and Asakura. I want you here. Your job is to hold Chokoji Castle. We are surround by clans who would love to sweep in while I'm gone and take everything I possess. I want you to stay here and guard the castle."

Shibata bowed deeply. He longed for the field of battle, but he would do what his lord ordered.

Shibata spent his days fortifying the castle. He set bamboo spikes around the perimeter and reinforced the gates. Day after day, he drilled the troops. All 400 samurai lived inside the castle keep. There they practiced their sword skills, and they stood watch. Every day was the same. They drilled, and they stood watch. Shibata wished desperately to be by his lord's side in pitched battle. But instead he watched the castle.

Then one day, the lookout at the top of the castle called down, "Dust cloud on the horizon." A runner took word to Shibata: "A dust cloud is approaching. It's big."

Shibata sent out scouts, and they came back with the news. The dust cloud was an army, the Rokkaku Yoshikata, a band of well-trained, dedicated samurai. Thousands of them marched toward the castle, 4000 it turned out. Two years earlier Oda had defeated the Rokkaku, and now they had come for revenge. They had one goal, to take Chokoji Castle.

Shibata closed the gates. He stationed the archers at the arrow slits. He ordered pots of sand and water to be heated in case the Rokkaku elected to scale the wall. He armed and armored his men, and he waited.

The Rokkaku, however, didn't attack. Instead, they stationed themselves outside the castle gate and waited. Shibata's archers took potshots at them from time to time, but the Rokkaku were just out of range. After dark, Shibata sent out small groups on raids behind enemy lines, but these raids were little more than bee stings to an army that large.

After a week or so of waiting, Shibata finally learned what the Rokkaku were waiting for. They had cut the castle aqueduct and were waiting for the water supply to dry up.

Shibata ordered all the remaining water in the castle to be gathered together into large clay pots. They would begin rationing. Shibata knew that their best hope was to last until Oda returned. But he had no idea when that would be.

By the end of the week, even with tight rationing, the castle was down to three large pots of water. For 400 people, that was one day's supply. Shibata sent spies into the enemy camp. They came back reporting that the Rokkaku knew how short the water was. The enemy planned to give Shibata and his men enough time to begin dying from dehydration. Then the Rokkaku would storm in and take the castle.

That evening as the sun set, Shibata pulled the lookouts from their posts. He took the archers from the arrow slits. He even removed the guards from the gates. He called for all 400 warriors to join him in the great courtyard. When all were assembled, Shibata mounted the platform.

"These three jars," he said, "are the last of the water."

The warriors murmured quietly. They had all been brought up on the story of the disgrace of Akasaka. According to the story, 282 warriors were barricaded in a castle with no water source. They lasted as long as they could, but finally their leader opened the front gates and led his men out to surrender to the enemy rather than die of thirst. For Shibata's warriors, who had been trained their whole lives to die before surrendering, the shame of Akasaka was as real as the three large pots sitting on the platform in front of them.

"It is a terrible thing to die of thirst," Shibata said. "That's why I am forced to take extreme measures."

Shibata picked up his spear. He motioned the guards guarding the water to move aside. Then he took the spear and one by one smashed the pots. The precious water flooded over the platform and onto the ground. It was only their rigorous training that kept the thirsty samurai from diving into the puddle to save what water they could before the earth took it all.

"There," Shibata said. "Now you are all dead. That leaves you with only two choices. Stay here and die of thirst like a dog panting in the sun. Stay here and hope death comes before you disgrace yourself by surrendering to the Rokkaku. Or come with me, engage the enemy right now, and die like a warrior."

The courtyard erupted. All the anger, fear, frustration, and uncertainty of the siege boiled over. The samurai shouted like caged beasts. They charged the gate. Shibata took his place at the front of them and ordered the gates opened.

The 400 charged out into the waiting 4,000 Rokkaku, catching them off guard just as they were falling asleep. The 400 swung their swords fearlessly, fighting like men with no fear of death, like men with nothing to lose. Their shouts set terror into the heart of the Rokkaku. Their fierceness caused the young, weak, and inexperienced to break first. But soon all the Rokkaku were bolting right and left. The 400 had to chase them down just to get them to engage.

The battle was so decisive that the Rokkaku clan never recovered. When Oda returned from defeating Asai and Asakura, he found Shibata and the remnants of his troops still guarding Chokoji Castle. The aqueduct was repaired. The lookout was atop the castle, and Chokoji was back to drilling his samurai, who had taken to calling him Oni Shibata after the oni, a mythical creature who fought like a demon.

When Oda heard the story, he promoted Shibata and gave him the province of Echizen, which Oda had taken from Asakura in battle. Shibata ruled his own province, but whenever Oda called, Shibata came and fought beside him in battle.

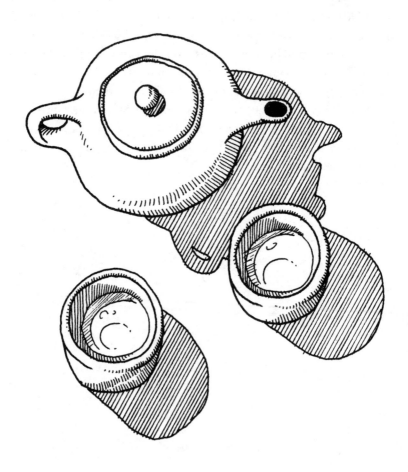

*I*n Japan, the tea ceremony, called the cha no yu, is an ancient tra-
dition. To perform the tea ceremony well, one must be completely
focused and aware but completely relaxed. Each movement is done with
beauty but also simplicity of movement. In that way, the cha no yu is
much like the martial arts. As in the martial arts, if people want to
learn the tea ceremony, they go to a tea master. The tea master teaches
not only the techniques of serving tea, but the art and self-control
needed to perform the ceremony with poise and focus.

A Tea Master Faces Death

A tea master, carrying a tray of cups and powdered tea, was walking
down the street one day. Suddenly, out of a nearby noodle shop, an angry
samurai burst into the street. The tea master was startled and jumped
back. But the samurai, who wasn't watching where he was going, ran
right into him. The tea master's tray overturned. The cups fell to the
ground, and the powdered tea spilled all over the samurai's sleeve.

"Watch where you're going," the samurai growled.

"My apologies, sir," the tea master replied, quickly trying to brush
the green powder from the samurai's sleeve.

"Stay away from me," said the samurai, pulling his sleeve away. The
tea master quickly withdrew his hand, but bumped the samurai's katana
handle in the process.

"You touched my sword!" The samurai's eyes blazed with anger.

"My apologies, sir." The tea master bowed his head.

"You touched my sword! If you wanted to offend me, why didn't
you just slap my face? That would be less of an insult than bumping my
sword!"

"But sir," said the tea master, "I didn't mean to touch your sword.
It was an accident. The whole thing was just an unfortunate accident. I
beg you to forgive me."

"It's too late for that now," the samurai replied. "My name is Genji.
I challenge you to a duel. Tomorrow evening. I will meet you in front of
my home. Bring a sword."

The samurai and his retainer swaggered off. The tea master stooped to pick up his cups with shaking hands. He did not even own a sword.

The tea master returned home to clean his cups and refill the tea box. Then he headed out again to the home of his student for that day. When he arrived late, his student, a wealthy nobleman, asked him where he had been. The tea master described his encounter with the samurai.

"You say his name was Genji?" the nobleman asked.

"Yes," said the tea master.

"And you will fight him?" the nobleman asked.

"I suppose I must," replied the tea master.

"Then you will die," said the nobleman, a look of sadness on his face. "Genji is a powerful fighter and not known for his mercy. If you fight him, he will kill you."

"Then we had better get on with your lesson," said the tea master. "It appears you will not get another one from me."

That evening, the tea master stopped by the shop of his friend the swordmaker. The two old friends sat together sipping sake like they had so many evening before.

"What's troubling you, my friend?" asked the sword maker.

"I need to buy one of your swords," said the tea master.

The sword maker smiled. "My friend," he said, "you could not afford one of my swords. Besides, since when do you need a sword?"

"Since this morning," said the tea master, taking another sip of his sake. He explained the situation to his friend who listened, barely breathing. "So you see," said the tea master, "I need a sword. I know it's a lot to ask but perhaps I could borrow one from you. I will ask Genji's retainers to make sure you get it back after the duel."

The sword maker was silent for a long time. The finality of his friend's words hung in the air between them.

"If you must die," the sword maker finally said, "why would you want to die as a poor sword fighter? If you must die, why don't you die as you have lived, as one of the greatest tea masters alive today?"

The tea master thought about this for a while. Then he rose, patted his friend on the shoulder, and without a word walked out into the night.

With a growing resolution in his heart, he walked across town to

Genji's house. At the gate he met one of Genji's retainers.

"Would you give your lord a message for me?" he said. "Please tell him that I will meet him tomorrow evening here in front of his home for our duel. But please ask him if he will meet me tomorrow afternoon in my teahouse. I wish to give him a final gift."

The next morning the tea master rose early to prepare for the samurai's arrival. He swept the path and tended the garden outside his teahouse. He carefully cleaned the table and utensils, and arranged a simple but elegant flower arrangement. Then he mindfully brushed his best kimono and put it on. With everything in place, he went to his front gate to await the samurai's arrival.

Around mid afternoon, the samurai and two retainers arrived. The tea master bowed to them.

"I'm so glad you could come," he said.

"My retainer tells me you wish to offer me a present," the samurai said, a mocking smile on his face. "Could you be offering me a bribe to spare your life?"

"No, of course not, sir," the tea master replied. "I would never think to insult you in such a way." He led the samurai to the door of the teahouse and motioned to a bench in the garden where the retainers could wait.

"Then if it's not to offer me a bribe, have you dragged me here to beg me to spare your life?"

"No," said the tea master. "I understand that your honor must be satisfied. All I ask is that you allow my last act to be an honorable one as well." He entered the teahouse and motioned for his guest to sit. "I am a tea master. The tea ceremony is not only what I do, but who I am. All I ask is that you allow me to perform it one last time for you."

The samurai didn't completely understand, but he kneeled and nodded to the tea master to begin.

Together they sat in the quiet simplicity of the teahouse. The rustle of the leaves on the trees outside was the only sound. The tea master opened his tea box, and the pungent smell of the green powder mingled with the smell of the flowers on the shelf.

Quietly, purposefully, the tea master scooped a small amount of tea into a cup. With a small ladle, he dipped hot water from a pot and poured it onto the tea. The samurai watched, caught up in the quiet intensity of the tea master's movements.

Taking a small whisk in one hand and the cup in the other, the tea master stirred the tea until it foamed. Then bowing with complete calmness of spirit, he handed the cup to the samurai.

The samurai drank. When he handed the cup back, the tea master's hands were completely steady, the look in his eyes utterly relaxed but aware.

"Thank you," said the tea master after the two had risen to leave. "I will go with you now to your home for our duel."

"Perhaps that won't be necessary," said the samurai. "I have never seen a man so calm and self-possessed before a duel. Today even I was excited and fearful, though I am sure I could kill you. But you were not only calm, you brought a calmness to me as well."

The tea master looked into the samurai's eyes, smiled, and bowed. The samurai returned the bow even more deeply.

"Master," the samurai said. "I cannot kill a man like you. The only thing I could honorably do to a man like you is to ask him to teach me. Will you instruct me in the ways of the tea ceremony?"

"Of course," said the tea master. "I will meet you in front of your home tomorrow at sunset."

*G*ogen Yamaguchi was the founder of the Goju-ryu style of karate. His nickname, "The Cat" referred not only to his long mane of hair, but to the way he was able to fight with the power and instincts of the big cats. During World War II, Yamaguchi worked for the Japanese government, which sent him into China on a special mission. While there, he was captured and put into a labor camp.

How Yamaguchi, Founder of Goju-ryu, Became "The Cat"

Yamaguchi was not like the other prisoners. He kept to himself. He did his work without complaining, was respectful to the guards, and did everything he was told. But when he had finished his work for the day, rather than spending time with the other prisoners, he would retreat to his cell. There he would stand motionless and begin to breathe. The guards and other prisoners would gradually gather at the window of his cell. What they saw inside was not a prisoner, beaten down and tired, but the face of a powerful, ancient warrior.

He began the kata he performed every day. The muscles of his arms tightened like thick ropes as he pulled them across the front of his chest. His legs were like the gnarled roots of a tree grabbing powerfully at the ground. His breath came from his mouth in a low, powerful "hhwoooh" that sent shivers up the spines of everyone in the cell block. And on his face was a look of total fierceness and perfect concentration.

The guards hated Yamaguchi. Maintaining order in a labor camp where the prisoners outnumbered the guards twenty to one was not easy. It involved the efficient use of force and terror. A frightened prisoner was easy to handle. And Yamaguchi seemed never to be frightened. That is why one day the commander of the prison camp gave the order, "Break him."

The guards knew their job well. They had broken many other prisoners before. They began by depriving Yamaguchi of his sleep. Every

ten minutes all night long they would walk by his cell and wake him up. But each day, Yamaguchi would work like a man fully rested. And each evening he would return to his cell and do kata.

It's the kata, the guards decided. If they could deprive him of his evening exercise, they would be able to break him. So they put him in the solitary confinement box. The box was small, barely tall enough for Yamaguchi to sit upright, too short to lie down, and so narrow that when he sat cross-legged his knees touched both sides. The guards handed in brown bread and water twice a day, but mostly they just let Yamaguchi sit.

In the box Yamaguchi sat quietly. He closed his eyes, stilled his breathing, watched it come into his body through his nose and leave his body through his mouth. He emptied his mind of thought, of pain, of anxiety and emotion. For hours each day he sat and meditated. When he wasn't meditating, he would sleep. Or he would do breathing and energy exercises. At all hours of the day and night, the guards would hear Yamaguchi's powerful "hhwoooh" filling the compound.

After several weeks, they let him out. Two guards stood ready to carry him back to his cell. Prisoners who had been in the box were always too stiff and weak to walk. But when they opened the door of the box, Yamaguchi crawled out under his own power, stood, bowed to the guards, and walked back to his cell. His color was good. And except for a little stiffness in his walk, he looked strong.

"He's a strong man," the guards said to each other. "But even a strong man can be broken." That night they dragged Yamaguchi from his cell and beat him. Though any normal man would have broken at their hands, Yamaguchi didn't even cry out in pain. His face was still, like the surface of a calm lake. His breathing was deep and regular. The look in his eyes was far away. When the guards finished, they had to bring him out of some kind of trancelike state to get him to walk back to his cell.

The beating went on for days. But each time, Yamaguchi would retreat inside himself, leaving the blows to fall on a hollow shell. Finally, the guards decided the beatings were not working. Sleep deprivation hadn't worked. The solitary box hadn't worked. The man was a warrior like they had never seen before. Perhaps they would be able to use that fact.

Several days after the beatings stopped, a truck rolled into the labor camp. On it was a large cage. In the cage was a tiger. A dozen guards unloaded the cage from the truck and placed it in the center of the compound.

The commander came out of his office to inspect the beast. The tiger was huge, full grown, not young, but certainly not too old to dispose of a puny human being. The commandant ordered that the tiger not be given anything to eat for the next three days. After that, the whole camp would watch as Yamaguchi became the tiger's breakfast.

The tiger paced his cage, clearly in a bad mood. The prisoners stood in tight lines along one side of the compound. The guards brought Yamaguchi out of his cell.

"Strip him," the commander ordered. The guards removed all Yamaguchi's clothes.

It was the perfect plan. If Yamaguchi wanted to avoid the pain of being ripped to shreds, he would have to enter a trance. But if he entered a trance, he wouldn't be facing death like a warrior. Either way, the other prisoners would see that any man, even a man like Yamaguchi, could be broken.

Two guards prodded the tiger with sticks, backing it into the rear of its cage. Another guard undid the latch and opened the door. The guards on either side of Yamaguchi made ready to shove him through the door. But Yamaguchi shook loose from their grip, straightened his shoulders, and walked through the door of the cage on his own.

The look on Yamaguchi's face was the same intense concentration and fierceness as he displayed so many times before in his katas. He stood before the tiger without a sign of fear. For a moment, the tiger froze. Was it afraid?

The tiger pounced. Yamaguchi sidestepped and tapped the tiger square on the nose with a kick. The tiger shook his head and sneezed, giving Yamaguchi the split second he needed to get around the side. He landed an elbow on the tiger's ear, then climbed onto its back. The tiger twisted its body, trying to sink its teeth into the man who clung to its back like a tick. But Yamaguchi held tight, gripping the tiger's back with his knees, squeezing the tiger's throat tight against his forearm. The tiger's eyes went wild with alarm. It threw its head back and swiped at the air with its claws, but Yamaguchi stuck to it like a second skin.

Gradually, the tiger's movements became less sharp. Then its eyes glazed over, and it sunk like an empty sack to the floor of the cage. Yamaguchi clung to it still, waiting, listening. Finally he let go, climbed off the tiger's back, and stood.

A guard moved to unlatch the cage. Yamaguchi turned to look at him. The guard looked deep into the warrior's eyes and spun on his heel and ran. Yamaguchi turned to scan the crowd of prisoners. As his eyes fell upon them, they moved back in fear. In his eyes they could still see the fight, the energy, the power. The guards ordered everyone back to their cells while six of them removed Yamaguchi at gunpoint from the unconscious tiger's cage.

Less than a week later, a truck drove into the compound. The Japanese government had arranged for a prisoner exchange. Yamaguchi was going home. As the guards escorted him onto the truck and watched it drive out of the compound, they knew that they had met one of the rarest creatures on earth, a man who could not be broken.

*S*okon Matsumura, who also appears in "A Karate Master Fights a Bull," was one of Okinawa's most famous martial artists. His wife, Yonamine Chiru, was also a martial artist, but we know less about her. We know that she came from a family of renowned fighters, that she was strong and talented, and she had a mind of her own. Some of her legends are too fantastic to be true. However, we do know that in at a time when women were expected to be quiet and demure, Matsumura loved his wife not despite her talents and strengths but because of them.

A Karate Master's Love of a Strong Woman

"Her family has money," one of Matsumura's buddies offered.

"Not enough for me," another said. "I mean can you imagine?" The three of them sat around a table waiting for the server to bring their meal.

"I saw her once," the first buddy said. "She was sweeping a floor. This sack of rice was in the way. So she picks it up. With one hand, she picks it up to sweep underneath. The thing had to weigh a hundred pounds. And she picks it up like it's nothing." He mimed holding a sack straight out in front of him.

Matsumura took a sip of his drink and smiled a little.

"But at least she did that at home," the second buddy said. "She's always challenging people. Out in public."

"Men," the first said, correcting him.

"Yeah, she's always challenging men. Full contact, bare knuckle *tode*, arm wrestling, weightlifting. Even sumo! She'll challenge anyone to any feat of strength. And she wins. A lot of the time she wins." He shook his head.

"Can you imagine having a wife like that? It's no wonder she's not married."

"She's not married?" Matsumura looked up, suddenly interested.

"Of course, she's not," the first buddy said. "Who'd have a wife like that?"

"I would," Matsumura said. "In a heartbeat." His friends stared at him. "I like strong women," he said, shrugging.

"But what if she's good enough to beat you up? Would you like it if she could beat you up?"

"So what if she can?" Matsumura said. "I can beat most people up. But just because I *can* doesn't mean I *do*. As far as I'm concerned, skill is skill. I don't care if you're male or female, martial arts skill does not come easily. I respect anyone who has worked hard enough to get that good. What's her name?"

"Yonamine Tsuru. They call her Chiru."

"Isn't her father a martial artist?" Matsumura asked.

"Yup," his buddy replied. "Do you want to meet her? I could arrange it."

"Certainly," Matsumura said. "In fact, I wouldn't mind fighting her. Could you arrange that?"

"You're crazy. You know that, don't you?"

Matsumura just shrugged.

The fight was at Chiru's father's dojo. Matsumura's friends had arranged it, and then they accompanied him to the dojo. They couldn't believe he would go through with it. But there they were. His buddies took a seat on the edge of the floor.

Matsumura and Chiru didn't even exchange pleasantries. They bowed. Matsumura waited, let Chiru make the first move. She obliged with a jab so fast, Matsumura barely blocked it before it struck him in the nose. He put in a few light strikes, which Chiru blocked easily. Then she countered with a cross-body punch to his ribs that took his breath for a moment. After that, Matsumura stopped seeing this a lark, and he started fighting in earnest.

After the fight, Matsumura's buddies couldn't decide who fought better. Matsumura believed he could beat her in a real fight. He had pulled some of his punches like he would with any sparring partner who was smaller than he was. But he had to admit that he could still feel some of the places she'd hit him. He would be black and blue in the morning.

That next morning, with bruises beginning to rise, Matsumura rose early. He bathed carefully, and put on his best clothes. He walked to Chiru's house and asked to see her parents. As they sat together drinking tea, Matsumura explained that he was a military man and that he worked for the king. He would never be rich, but he respected their daughter. Then he asked to marry Chiru. Her parents said yes.

The marriage was unusual but good. Matsumura and Chiru trained together. Sometimes they sparred, sometimes lifted weights. They pushed each other to work harder. For even though he liked strong women, Matsumura secretly still wanted to be stronger than Chiru was. It was good motivation for him. Secretly, Chiru also wondered if she could become stronger than Matsumura.

One day the two of them got into an argument after sparring. Matsumura had a black eye, and Chiru had a sprained finger. They were both battling their anger.

"You are good," Matsumura said. "But sparring is sparring. A fight on the battlefield is a completely different thing from sparring."

"I doubt the king would be willing to accept me as one of his soldiers," Chiru said, "so we are unlikely to find out what I could do on the battlefield."

"Yes," but a self-defense situation is the same," Matsumura said. "Fighting off bandits is different from sparring, too."

"You don't think I could defend myself against bandits?" she asked.

"Maybe you could. Maybe you couldn't," Matsumura said. "I'm just saying that sparring is not the same as the real thing."

Chiru turned on her heel and strode off to the house. Matsumura decided he needed to show her what he meant.

"This sounds like a really bad idea," his buddy said.

"I can't believe you talked me into it," his brother added. They were blackening their faces to blend in with the night.

"Put more of that stuff on your forehead," Matsumura said. "If she recognizes us, it won't be a fair test."

"So let me make sure I have this right," his buddy said. "We disguise ourselves and hide in the bushes. When Chiru comes by on her way home, we pretend to be bandits and jump her. The three of us completely overpower her. Then when we have her on the ground, you reveal who you are and then…what? You win this silly argument?"

"Then she recognizes that sparring is not a real fight," Matsumura said. "She recognizes the limits of her skills. It's important that she do that. If she thinks she can dispatch a bandit just because she can beat some guy in the dojo, one of these days she's going to get hurt."

"I still think it's a bad idea," his brother said.

"It will work," Matsumura said.

Chiru heard them before she walked by the bush. She knew there were more than one, but she couldn't tell how many. She shifted her bundle to her left hand, and got a tight grip on the bucket in her right. She pasted a clueless look on her face and strode past the bush.

They pounced. Chiru threw the bundle at one of them, and swung the bucket and caught the closest attacker on the side of the head. He went down with a moan. She followed through and backhanded the bucket up into the second attacker's jaw. He stumbled a bit and then backed away, his lip bleeding and his hands held up in surrender.

The third attacker rushed her, going for a low tackle. It was Matsumura. He had some black grease rubbed on his face, but she would know her husband even with a bag over his head. Chiru sidestepped at the last moment and swept Matsumura's feet out from under him. He fell on his hands and knees. Chiru whipped off her belt and wrapped it around his neck. Careful not to do any permanent damage, she tightened it enough to get his attention. He froze.

"On the ground," she said, tweaking the belt just a little tighter. Matsumura complied. Chiru tied off the belt with a slip knot around his neck. Then she grabbed Matsumura's wrists and wrapped the other end of the belt around them as well. Rolling him onto his side, she untied his belt and wrapped it around herself. Picking up her bucket and bundle, she headed home.

Matsumura came into the house. Chiru was working in the kitchen, wearing his belt.

"How is your brother?" she asked.

"He's…fine," Matsumura said. Did she know?

Chiru eyed his open jacket. "I believe this is yours," she said untying the belt and handing it to him. Matsumura sighed. Reaching into his sleeve he pulled out her belt and handed it to her. "And this is yours," he said.

Chiru smiled quietly to herself and went back to her cooking.

Though tae kwon do is a relatively modern martial art, the roots of Korean martial arts extend hundreds of years into the past. The old-style Korean martial art was called Taekyon. Duk Ki Song was one of the last people to study Taekyon. But through his student, Han Il Dong, elements of the ancient Korean way of fighting were passed to Hong Hi Choi, the "father of modern tae kwon do."

How Loyalty Saved Korean Martial Arts

"Taekyon is dead," Hue Lim sighed. He was in one of his dark moods. "Children think it's just a game to play at youth festivals. Thugs learn just enough to beat on their victims. But nobody practices the true art anymore."

"We do, master," Duk replied quietly. "You and I do."

"Yes," his teacher replied. "You and I do. But sometimes I feel like we're the only ones."

"But so long as we do, the art will continue to live, right?"

Duk's teacher looked into his young face. His new student was thirteen and eager to learn. But more than that he had an aptitude for the martial arts that was rare. Hue Lim nodded his head.

"You're right. So long as one person is willing to teach, and another person is willing to learn, Taekyon isn't dead yet."

"Are the rumors true?" Duk asked his teacher. "A boy at school said the Japanese are going to outlaw all martial arts in Korea."

"It's true," Hue Lim said.

"But they can't do that," Duk complained. "I haven't learned the advanced kicks yet."

Hue Lim smiled at his student. In the last two years, Duk had become a very capable young student. At fifteen years old, he was almost as tall as his teacher. Hue Lim knew that with Duk's focus and self-discipline he could be a great Taekyon artist.

"Do you really think the Japanese government cares about your ability to kick?" Hue Lim replied.

"No," Duk replied. He hung his head. "But can't we do something? Can't you keep teaching me secretly? We could practice at night."

"And if the police come by and look over the fence, they will see us. Or hear us. Or someone will tell them. And they will come and lock us up." Hue Lim looked his student in the eye. "I can't do that to you," he said. "I can't do something that would put you in jail."

"I'm not afraid to go to jail," Duk protested. "I'm willing to take the risk."

"Duk," Hue Lim replied. "I am your teacher. It's my choice."

"I'm sorry, teacher," Duk said quietly. "Of course that is your choice. I'm sorry. But if you stop teaching, and I stop learning, then Taekyon really will be dead, won't it?"

Hue Lim did not reply. He sighed deeply. "Go home, Duk. There is nothing we can do."

Duk turned to leave, tears in his eyes.

Now and then, Hue Lim and Duk would meet. Hue Lim would show his student a few moves from a Korean Youth Festival game. Duk recognized the moves as Taekyon in disguise. He practiced them every day. Sometimes he would even find a quiet place where no one could see him, and he would throw punches and kicks until he could hardly stand. He would take out his anger against the ban on a sack filled with sand, honing his technique in secret. But he knew that without a teacher, his skill would never fully develop. He longed for the day when he could study Taekyon in the open again.

One day, a few months after the ban began, Hue Lim came to Duk with news.

"I'm leaving," Hue Lim informed his pupil.

"Where are you going?" Duk asked, trying not to let the shock and sadness creep into his voice.

"I'm going to a Buddhist temple not far from here. I've heard rumors that some Taekyon fighters have gathered there to study and teach."

"You're leaving to teach someone else? You won't be teaching me any more?" Duk's voice quivered, despite his best efforts.

"Well, I was hoping you would come with me. We would live at the monastery, and you would train as my apprentice. Someday when the ban is lifted, you can teach Taekyon."

"And if one person is willing to teach, and another person is willing to learn, the art will continue to live, right?"

"Right," said Hue Lim. "Go pack your things."

Taekyon continued to be outlawed for thirty-six years. Duk Ki Song continued to study, then to teach. In 1945 the ban was lifted. By that time, he was one of only two Taekyon teachers still living. He began teaching in public again. Koreans began studying martial arts again, but most of them studied Chinese and Japanese arts.

Shortly after the ban was lifted, Duk Ki Song gave a Taekyon demonstration at a birthday party for South Korean president Sung-Man Yi. Korean martial artists who saw the demonstration were impressed with Taekyon's powerful circular kicks. Within twenty years, tae kwon do had incorporated those kicks into their arsenal. Though Taekyon has died as a separate martial art, it lives on as a part of tae kwon do.

*K*yudo is traditional Japanese archery. Kyudo archers use a very long bow—some kyudo bows are seven and a half feet long. They shoot long, lightweight arrows at a stationary target between 85 and 180 feet away.

Kyudo, like many of the martial arts, trains students not just in technique but in awareness and spirit. A kyudo archer strives for a calm, balanced exterior and a powerful, single-minded spirit. Students of kyudo believe that an archer's spirit is reflected in the sound the bow makes when the arrow is released.

A Kyudo Master Makes a Bet

For as long as he could remember, all Saito ever wanted to do was to become an expert archer in the service of his lord. For ten years, since he was three years old, he had been practicing with the bow. Soon he would be old enough to join his father in the daimyō's fighting forces.

One afternoon, Saito was in a meadow outside town shooting with two of his friends. The meadow was ideal for shooting because it lay at the base of a tall cliff. If the arrows missed the target, they would bounce off the cliff and not be lost. The boys took turns naming a target and trying to hit it. Saito was happy. Nothing made him feel better than the sound of his arrow hitting the target, and that day his arrows were hitting nearly every time.

As the boys practiced, a stranger walked by on the road. He spotted the three boys, waved, and stopped to watch.

Saito loved an audience. He winked at his friends and quickly—one, two, three—put three arrows into the tree he was shooting at.

"That's very accurate shooting," the stranger called out as he walked toward the boys.

"Yes," said Saito.

The stranger raised an eyebrow at Saito's reply. "Are you always that accurate?" he asked.

"Almost always," Saito replied. "I am studying to be an archer in the service of my daimyō. Accuracy is crucial in battle."

"I see," said the stranger. "And have you ever been in battle?"

"No," Saito admitted. "But I can shoot from atop a horse. I can shoot birds in midflight. I always hit what I aim at. I'll do fine in battle."

"Mmm," said the stranger neither agreeing nor disagreeing. "Let's see you hit that tree." He pointed at a tree about fifty feet away.

Saito pulled an arrow from his quiver and hit the tree easily. The stranger walked over to the tree, pulled out the arrow. He reached into his bag and pulled out a small piece of cloth, which he wedged into a space in the bark. Returning to Saito, he handed him the arrow. "Follow me," the stranger said walking still farther from the tree. When they were about 150 feet away, the stranger said, "Shoot from here."

Saito set the arrow on the string, pulled it back, and without even a pause for aim, released it. The arrow flew true and pinned the cloth to the tree.

"That was easy," Saito said. "Let me do a harder one." He scanned the meadow until he saw a rock sticking up a few feet above the grass. Trotting off, he climbed the slippery surface. Perched atop it he fitted another arrow. He fired, and again hit the cloth squarely.

"Would you like to see me shoot a bird?" Saito asked. "A target's a lot more fun if it's moving."

"No," said the stranger. "But there is something I'll bet you can't shoot."

"What?" said Saito. "If it can be hit with an arrow, I can hit it."

"I'll bet you can't hit the trunk of that tree over there," the stranger pointed to a large tree with a wide trunk over by the base of the cliff. "I'll bet you can't hit it from a hundred feet."

"I'll take that bet," Saito said. "What are we betting?"

"I get to choose where you stand," the stranger said.

"Yes, yes," said Saito, "no problem. What are we betting?"

"If you hit the trunk of the tree below the lowest branch with your first arrow, I will buy you a new bow. If you do not hit the trunk with your first arrow, you will come to my house every afternoon for a year, and I will put you to work."

Saito grinned then bowed. "You, sir, have a bet," he said.

"Very well," said the stranger, "follow me."

The three boys were huffing and panting by the time they reached the top of the cliff. They looked down over the meadow they had just been in, down over the town and the surrounding area. Saito saw the target tree about seventy-five feet below them. The trunk was clearly visible. The stranger had underestimated him. He'd shot from heights like this before. It would be no problem hitting the trunk from this distance.

"The new bow is as good as mine," he whispered to his friend. His friend smiled back and nodded.

"Very good," said the stranger looking over the cliff. "This will do nicely."

"All right," said Saito, pulling an arrow from his quiver and setting it on his string. He was about to pull it back when the stranger put a hand on his shoulder.

"Wait," he said. "Remember, I get to choose where you stand." Saito returned the arrow to his quiver.

The stranger walked along the edge of the cliff, obviously looking for something. A small, flat boulder caught his attention. He nudged it with his foot. It rocked slightly. He stepped up onto it. It shifted and slipped. Saito caught his breath, fearing it would topple over the edge. It held, but barely. The stranger stepped down.

"This is the place I choose," he said, point to the boulder. "Shoot from here, atop the rock."

Saito's smile faded. He walked to the edge cliff and looked down. His toe caught some loose gravel. It clattered over the edge and bounced down the cliff. The tree looked suddenly smaller. "But if I fell," Saito said, "I might be killed."

"Oh, yes," the stranger said. "I'd say you would certainly be killed."

Saito stared at the rock. He tested it with his hand. It rocked, its front edge dipping down over the precipice. He shot a glance at his friends. They stood motionless, their eyes wide. A look of resolution came over Saito's face.

"I'll do it," he said. Slowly, deliberately he approached the rock, drawing the arrow from his quiver again. He stepped his first foot onto the rock. The wind caught the tip of his bow and tugged at it gently. The boulder shifted slightly under his weight. Saito froze.

"There's the whip of the string to think about," he said, his foot still gingerly resting atop the boulder. "Let me think for a moment here."

"Yes," said the stranger. "There is the whip to consider. But it would be no different from the shot you took from on top of the rock down there." Saito's eyes again went to the meadow. It seemed to swim below him.

Carefully he edged his second foot into place. Slowly he drew his bow. The wind gusted. Saito scrambled back to safety.

"It was a silly bet in the first place," he muttered putting the arrow back in his quiver.

"Yes, it was, wasn't it?" the stranger replied. "But that doesn't really matter given that we both gave our word." Saito looked into his eyes. He was serious.

"Yes," Saito said. "I gave my word. I will come to your house each afternoon for a year to work for you. It beats falling over this cliff."

The stranger smiled. "I suppose it does. Now before we go down, may I ask a favor?" he said. "May I borrow your bow and an arrow?"

Saito nodded and handed him his bow and the arrow he had just put back into his quiver. The stranger bowed deeply as he received it. He turned, walked to the edge of the cliff, and climbed atop the rock. Carefully, he drew the bow, then paused and waited. Almost imperceptibly, the string released itself. It whipped against the upper part of the bow with a crisp, clear sound. The arrow flew.

Saito and his friends stepped to the edge of the cliff and cautiously peered down. There was the arrow protruding out of the exact center of the tree trunk.

"All this time you have been shooting to improve your aim," said the stranger backing away from the cliff. "Come to my house tomorrow when the sun is low on the horizon. I'll introduce you to my other kyudo students. Then you can begin shooting to improve yourself."

"*Fifty Thousand High Blocks*" is a modern story. It is based, however, on an ancient practice—a test of the student's patience. Some teachers made students wait weeks or even years before they would take them on as students. Other teachers would ask students to do chores for several weeks or months before teaching them martial arts. Other teachers would ask students to repeat a single technique over and over before giving them a new technique. These tests were not as cruel as they may seem at first glance. They were, rather, the teachers' way of seeing whether the new student had the patience and self-control to begin learning the martial arts. They knew that the martial arts, like many new skills, require years of patient repetition to master. They knew that to learn to fight meant first to learn perseverance.

Fifty Thousand High Blocks

A young woman who wanted to learn to defend herself sought a martial arts teacher to teach her. She rode her bicycle to a nearby kung fu school, and asked the teacher for lessons.

"Are you willing to practice?" the teacher asked.

"Of course," said the young woman.

"Good," said the teacher. "Your first task is to learn to punch. Do it like this." He showed the young woman the first basic punch. He worked with her until her technique was correct. Then he stepped off the training floor. "What I want you to do is practice the punch fifty thousand times. When you have finished, let me know."

The young woman watched the teacher leave. Fifty thousand times! That would take her days. When the teacher was out of sight, she snuck out the door, got on her bike, and rode down the street.

After a short ride, she saw a tae kwon do school. She parked her bike, went inside, and asked the teacher to teach her.

"Are you willing to practice?" the teacher asked.

"Of course," said the young woman.

"Good," said the teacher. "Your first task is to learn to kick. Do it

one...

like this." She showed the young woman a basic front kick. She worked with her until her technique was correct. Then she stepped off the training floor. "What I want you to do is practice this kick fifty thousand times. When you have finished, let me know."

This time the young woman thought perhaps she might try to do the kick fifty thousand times. She counted ten, twenty, fifty, a hundred. After the hundredth kick, she decided she would never be able to do a thousand kicks much less fifty thousand. She snuck off the training floor and went out to her bike.

After a short ride, she came upon a karate school. Maybe this teacher could teach her to fight without so much repetition. She parked her bike, went inside, and asked the teacher to teach her.

"Are you willing to practice?" the teacher asked.

"Of course," said the young woman.

"Good," said the teacher. "Your first task is to learn to block. Do it like this." He showed the young woman a basic high block. He worked with her until her technique was correct. Then he stepped off the training floor. "What I want you to do is practice this block fifty thousand times. When you have finished, let me know."

The young woman was disappointed. This teacher was just like the others. But she really wanted to learn to defend herself, so she began to practice the block. She counted a hundred, two hundred, three hundred. At four hundred blocks she was positive that she understood the technique. She went to the teacher.

"Teacher," she said. "I'm ready to learn something new."

"Good," said the teacher. "Have you done the high block fifty thousand times?"

"Yes," the young woman lied.

"Fine," said the teacher. "Come with me." She brought the young woman to a beautifully made weapon rack. The young woman looked at the handcrafted tonfa, nunchaku, and eiku. This is more like it, the young woman thought to herself. I would love to learn to handle one of these fine weapons.

"Reach up to the shelf on top of the rack," her teacher said. "On the shelf you will find a bo, a long staff. We'll need it for your next lesson."

The young woman reached up to the shelf. It was far above her head. Standing on tiptoe, she felt around until she felt the bo with the very tips of her fingers. She rolled it forward carefully, but as it rolled over the front lip of the shelf, it slipped through her fingers and dropped. She scrambled to catch it, but it fell, hitting her squarely on the top of her head.

"That's strange," the teacher said. "Most people after fifty thousand high blocks would have blocked that bo automatically."

The young woman felt her ears grow red with embarrassment. "I didn't exactly finish the fifty thousand," she said.

"I didn't think so," said the teacher. He picked up the bo from the floor, replaced it on the shelf, and walked off the training floor. The young woman rubbed the growing knot on her head, and began doing high blocks.